The (Family) Pocket Promise Book

LARRY & NORDIS CHRISTENSON

Consulting Editors

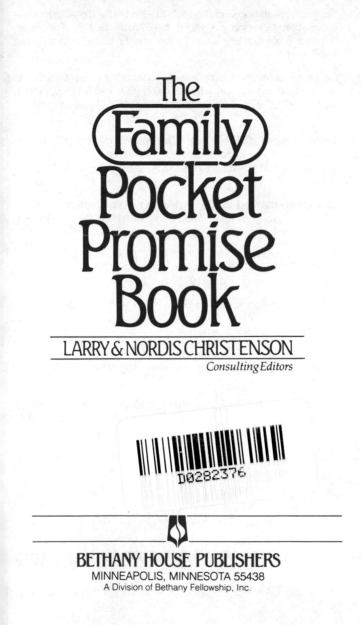

BETHANY HOUSE PUBLISHERS
MINNEAPOLIS, MINNESOTA 55438
A Division of Bethany Fellowship, Inc.

Scripture quotations marked NIV are from The Holy Bible, New International Version, copyright © 1978, by the New York International Bible Society. Used by permission of Zondervan Bible Publishers.

Scripture quotations from the New American Standard Bible, © The Lockman Foundation 1960, 1962, 1963, 1968, 1971, 1972, 1973, 1975, 1977, are marked NASB. Used by permission.

Verses marked NEB are from *The New English Bible*. © The Delegates of the Oxford University Press and The Syndics of the Cambridge University Press, 1961, 1970. Reprinted by permission.

Quotations marked BECK are from The New Testament in the Language of Today © 1963 Concordia Publishing House. Used by permission.

Scripture quotations taken from the *Good News Bible*, the Bible in Today's English Version, are marked TEV. Copyright © American Bible Society, 1976. Used by permission.

Scripture verses marked TLB are taken from The Living Bible, copyright © 1971 by Tyndale House Publishers, Wheaton, IL. Used by permission.

Scripture verses marked RSV are taken from the Revised Standard Version of the Bible, copyright 1946, 1952 © 1971, 1973. Used by permission.

Verses from The New Testament in Modern English, Revised Edition—J. B. Phillips, translator © J. B. Phillips 1958, 1960, 1972 are marked accordingly. Used by permission.

PREFACE

"All scripture is inspired by God and is profitable for teaching, for reproof, for correction, and for training in righteousness, that the man of God may be complete, equipped for every good work" (2 Tim. 3:16, 17).

But often we don't know what the Scripture says about a specific subject. Either we have not studied the appropriate passages, or at the time we studied them we did not need that word, so we did not "catch" the practical meaning. Or, we recall a verse but can't locate it in the Bible.

This book organizes appropriate Scripture verses about many different topics which concern our family lives. When you face a question, a problem, or a temptation, this handy source can help you find and read what the Scripture says about that topic.

Reading and pondering what God says in Scripture about a matter which is concerning us gives the Holy Spirit a powerful tool to work with in our lives. "Thy word have I hid in mine heart, that I might not sin against thee" (Ps. 119:11). God's Word is the raw material which the Holy Spirit uses to accomplish His purpose in our lives by:

1. *Teaching us God's ways.* The ways of God are not our ways. We need to learn them. "Show me thy ways, O Lord; teach me thy paths. Lead me in thy truth and teach me: for thou art the God of my salvation" (Ps. 25:4, 5). In this day of moral and social confusion, the

Bible remains a sure guide for teaching us God's ways, showing us God's mind.

2. *Reproving us.* God, the Holy Spirit, can reprove us, can convince us of sin, if we know what the Bible says about it. We need a standard outside of ourselves and outside of our worldly milieu to help us recognize sin. Sin is deceitful (Heb. 3:13). Often we do not *feel* that our sin is wrong. Our emotions can deceive us.

At one time in my life I was tempted in an area that I knew, intellectually, was sin, but I did not *feel* it was wrong and my feeling was stronger than my intellectual consent. I prayed, "God, show me what You think of this." In the next weeks many Bible verses about this topic came to me through my daily Bible reading, through Bible study, through Scripture reading in the Sunday services. God said it *was* sin. The Holy Spirit used those verses to convince me of sin so that I could agree with God and say, "This thing in my life is sin." If we agree with Him, He will take care of it (1 John 1:9). If we admit the sin He will forgive that sin, break its power in our lives, and take it away.

3. *Correcting us.* Some psychologies in our day have the effect of rationalizing sin; they convince us that everyone is doing it so it isn't wrong, or that it is someone else's fault so there is nothing to be done about it. God's attitude is different. He has *mercy* on us. He doesn't want us to carry sin and guilt. That's why He sent Jesus.

Jesus was obedient even to death so that He could break sin's power and set us free. He said to the woman whom He forgave, "Go, and sin no more." In other words, "Go, and quit doing this." And when He tells us that, He gives His Holy Spirit to enable us to obey. He gives us faith to obey ("the obedience of faith"—Rom. 1:5).

Jesus does not save us just so He can forgive us as He watches us sin again and again. He wants to show us the way out. Obedience is not legalism. Jesus expects that if we have faith, we will obey. And because the Holy Spirit is working Jesus' life in us to renew us, we can obey.

Many Christians look for a burst of evangelism, a spiritual renewal, to break upon the world in the 1980's. This won't happen unless God, the Holy Spirit, convicts of sin, and leads us into righteousness (John 16:8).

In the 1950's and 1960's many people answered a call of God during the Billy Graham Crusades. But the world we live in is very different from what the world was then. At that time our society supported faithfulness in marriage and the sanctity of human life. It recognized the destructiveness of perversion and addiction. This is no longer true. Today our nation is sinking into gross sin— sins of addiction, sexual immorality, self-centeredness, and unfaithfulness in all sorts of relationships. Only repentance and God-sent *renewal* can turn us back from the destruction we have chosen. Genuine repentance must precede renewal of the Church. This book can be a tool toward that goal.

4. *Training us in righteousness.* Even after repentance and turning from sin, we need the power and work of God, the Holy Spirit, in time of temptation to keep us from returning to sin. To be tempted is not sin, but temptation signals danger—like the road sign that says, "Danger Ahead."

One way to defeat temptation is to use the Word of God, which is "sharper than any two-edged sword" (Heb. 4:12). Suppose that a thought of temptation comes to mind (e.g., the thought that you want to eat something when you don't *need* to eat—in fact, you need *not* to eat). Recognizing this as temptation and finding an appropriate Scripture verse can bring God's Word directly to bear on the situation. In this instance, you might use the verse that Jesus himself quoted to the devil, "Man shall not live by bread alone" (Matt. 4:4).

As this book helps us find Scripture verses that deal with our specific needs, we can become, as St. Paul says, "washed" in the Word (Eph. 5:26). To be washed by the Word is a living reality available to us today. This book can help us experience it.

Larry and Nordis Christenson

TABLE OF CONTENTS

I. THE OCCULT

Some of my friends are peering into the future by astrology and various kinds of divination (Ouija board, tarot cards, I Ching sticks, Kreskin's pendulum, etc.). Some of these seem to really work. Does the Bible have anything to say about them?

1. "Do not practice divination or sorcery." (Lev. 19:26, NIV)

2. Let no one be found among you who sacrifices his son or daughter in the fire, who practices divination or sorcery, interprets omens, engages in witchcraft, or casts spells, or who is a medium or spiritist or who consults the dead. Anyone who does these things is detestable to the Lord, and because of these detestable practices the Lord your God will drive out those nations before you. (Deut. 18:10-12, NIV)

3. The nations you will dispossess listen to those who practice sorcery or divination. But as for you, the Lord your God has not permitted you to do so. (Deut. 18:14, NIV)

4. All the counsel you have received has only worn you out! Let your astrologers come forward, those stargazers

who make predictions month by month, let them save you from what is coming upon you. Surely they are like stubble; the fire will burn them up. They cannot even save themselves from the power of the flame. Here are no coals to warm anyone; here is no fire to sit by. (Isa. 47:13, 14, NIV)

5. Thus saith the Lord, Learn not the way of the heathen and be not dismayed at the signs of heaven; for the heathen are dismayed at them. For the customs of the people are vain. . . . (Jer. 10:2, 3, KJV)

And the Lord shall guide thee continually, and satisfy thy soul in drought, and make fat thy bones: and thou shalt be like a watered garden, and like a spring of water, whose waters fail not. (Isa. 58:11, KJV)

I've heard that a person in our community is a medium who talks with spirits. Is this one of God's ways of speaking to us?

1. "Do not turn to mediums or seek out spiritists, for you will be defiled by them. I am the Lord your God." (Lev. 19:31, NIV)

2. "I will set my face against anyone who consults mediums and wizards instead of me and I will cut that person off from his people." (Lev. 20:6, TLB)

3. Let no one be found among you who sacrifices his son or daughter in the fire, who practices divination or sorcery, interprets omens, engages in witchcraft, or casts spells, or who is a medium or spiritist or who consults the dead. Anyone who does these things is detestable to the Lord, and because of these detestable practices the Lord your God will drive out those nations before you. (Deut. 18:10-12, NIV)

4. And when they say to you, "Consult the mediums and the wizards who chirp and mutter," should not a people consult their God? Should they consult the dead on behalf of the living? To the teaching and to the testimony! (Isa. 8:19, 20, RSV)

I've noticed a lot of books in the library about magic, spells, charms and witchcraft. Is it all right if I just read some of them?

1. "Do not practice divination or sorcery." (Lev. 19:26, NIV)

2. "I will set my face against anyone who consults mediums and wizards instead of me and I will cut that person off from his people." (Lev. 20:6, TLB)

3. Let no one be found among you who sacrifices his son or daughter in the fire, who practices divination or sorcery, interprets omens, engages in witchcraft, or casts spells, or who is a medium or spiritist or who consults the dead. Anyone who does these things is detestable to the Lord, and because of these detestable practices the Lord

your God will drive out those nations before you. (Deut. 18:10-12, NIV)

4. The nations you will dispossess listen to those who practice sorcery or divination. But as for you, the Lord your God has not permitted you to do so. (Deut. 18:14, NIV)

5. "Therefore this is what the Sovereign Lord says: I am against your magic charms with which you ensnare people like birds." (Ezek. 13:20, NIV)

6. Now the works of the flesh are plain: fornication, impurity, licentiousness, idolatry, sorcery. (Gal. 5:19, 20, RSV)

7. Dear brothers, you are only visitors here. Since your real home is in heaven I beg you to keep away from the evil pleasures of this world; they are not for you, for they fight against your very souls. (1 Pet. 2:11, TLB)

8. But the cowardly, the unbelieving, the vile, the murderers, the sexually immoral, those who practice magic arts, the idolaters and all liars—their place will be in the fiery lake of burning sulfur. This is the second death. (Rev. 21:8, NIV)

If the other ways are wrong, how do I get God's guidance? How can I know God will show me what to do?

1. I will instruct you and teach you in the way you should

go; I will counsel you and watch over you. (Ps. 32:8, NIV)

2. You guide me with your counsel. (Ps. 73:24, NIV)

3. And the Lord will guide you continually, and satisfy you with all good things, and keep you healthy too; and you will be like a well-watered garden, like an ever-flowing spring. (Isa. 58:11, TLB)

4. If you want to know what God wants you to do, ask him, and he will gladly tell you, for he is always ready to give a bountiful supply of wisdom to all who ask him; he will not resent it. (James 1:5, TLB)

II. Sexual Problems

If two people love each other, why should they wait until marriage to engage in sexual intercourse?

1. Do you not know that the wicked will not inherit the kingdom of God? Do not be deceived: Neither the sexually immoral nor idolaters nor adulterers nor male prostitutes nor homosexual offenders . . . will inherit the kingdom of God. (1 Cor. 6:9, 10, NIV)

2. The body is not meant for sexual immorality, but for the Lord, and the Lord for the body. (1 Cor. 6:13, NIV)

3. Do you not know that your bodies are members of Christ himself? Shall I then take the members of Christ and unite them with a prostitute? Never! (1 Cor. 6:15, NIV)

4. Flee from sexual immorality. All other sins a man commits are outside his body, but he who sins sexually sins against his own body. (1 Cor. 6:18, NIV)

5. But among you there must not be even a hint of sexual immorality, or of any kind of impurity, or of greed, because these are improper for God's holy people. (Eph. 5:3, NIV)

6. For of this you can be sure: No immoral, impure or greedy person—such a man is an idolater—has any inheritance in the kingdom of Christ and of God. (Eph. 5:5, NIV).

7. Put to death, therefore, whatever belongs to your earthly nature: sexual immorality, impurity, lust, evil desires and greed, which is idolatry. But now you must rid yourselves of all such things as these. (Col. 3:5, 8, NIV)

8. Flee also youthful lusts: but follow righteousness; faith, charity, peace, with them that call on the Lord out of a pure heart. (2 Tim. 2:22, KJV)

9. In a similar way, Sodom and Gomorrah and the surrounding towns gave themselves up to sexual immorality and perversion. They serve as an example of those who suffer the punishment of eternal fire. (Jude 7, NIV)

10. But the cowardly, the unbelieving, the vile, the murderers, the sexually immoral, those who practice magic acts, the idolaters and all liars—their place will be in the fiery lake of burning sulfur. (Rev. 21:8, NIV)

I've read a book that says masturbation is just another way to have fun. God isn't against fun, is He?

1. "But I tell you that anyone who looks at a woman lustfully has already committed adultery with her in his heart." (Matt. 5:28, NIV)

2. "And if your right hand causes you to sin, cut it off and throw it away. It is better for you to lose one part of your body than for your whole body to go into hell." (Matt. 5:30, NIV)

3. Do not offer the parts of your body to sin, as instruments of wickedness, but rather offer yourselves to God, as those who have been brought from death to life; and offer the parts of your body to him as instruments of righteousness. (Rom. 6:13, NIV)

4. I put this in human terms because you are weak in your natural selves. Just as you used to offer the parts of your body in slavery to impurity and to ever-increasing wickedness, so now offer them in slavery to righteousness leading to holiness. When you were slaves to sin, you were free from the control of righteousness. What benefit did you reap at that time from the things you are now ashamed of? Those things result in death! (Rom. 6:19-21, NIV)

5. While we were living in the flesh, the Law stirred the sinful lusts in our organs into action to produce fruit for Death. But now that we have died to the Law which bound us, we are freed from it, not to serve in the old way under the Law but in the new way of the Spirit. (Rom. 7:5, 6, Beck)

6. Every test that you have experienced is the kind that normally comes to people. But God keeps his promise, and he will not allow you to be tested beyond your power to remain firm; at the time you are put to the test, he will give you the strength to endure it, and so provide you with a way out. (1 Cor. 10:13, TEV)

7. So whether you eat or drink or whatever you do, do it all for the glory of God. (1 Cor. 10:31, NIV)

8. But when you follow your own wrong inclinations your lives will produce these evil results: impure thoughts, eagerness for lustful pleasure ... envy, murder, drunkenness, wild parties, and all that sort of thing. Let me tell you again as I have before, that anyone living that sort of life will not inherit the kingdom of God. (Gal. 5:19, 21, TLB)

9. Since, then, you have been raised with Christ, set your hearts on things above, where Christ is seated at the right hand of God. Set your minds on things above, not on earthly things. (Col. 3:1, 2, NIV)

10. Put to death, therefore, whatever belongs to your earthly nature: sexual immorality, impurity, lust, evil desires and greed, which is idolatry. Because of these, the wrath of God is coming. You used to walk in these ways, in the life you once lived. But now you must rid yourselves of all such things as these. (Col. 3:5-8, NIV)

11. And whatever you do, in word or deed, do everything in the name of the Lord Jesus. (Col. 3:17, RSV)

12. Run from anything that gives you the evil thoughts that young men often have, but stay close to anything that makes you want to do right. Have faith and love, and enjoy the companionship of those who love the Lord and have pure hearts. (2 Tim. 2:22, TLB)

13. Dear friends, I urge you, as aliens and strangers in the world, to abstain from sinful desires, which war against your soul. (1 Pet. 2:11, NIV)

Whereby are given unto us exceeding great and precious promises: that by these ye might be partakers of the divine nature, having escaped the corruption that is in the world through lust. (2 Pet. 1:4, KJV)

Sometimes I get strange feelings that make me wonder if I'm a homosexual/lesbian. What should I do about these feelings?

1. "Homosexuality is absolutely forbidden, for it is an enormous sin." (Lev. 18:22, TLB)

2. They exchange the truth about God for a lie; they worship and serve what God has created instead of the Creator himself, who is to be praised for ever! Amen. Because they do this, God has given them over to shameful passions. Even the women pervert the natural use of their sex by unnatural acts. In the same way the men give up natural sexual relations with women and burn with passion for each other. Men do shameful things with each other, and as a result they bring upon themselves the punishment they deserve for their wrong doing.... Because those people refuse to keep in mind the true knowledge about God, he has given them over to corrupted minds, so that they do the things that they should not do. (Rom. 1:25-28, TEV)

3. Neither yield ye your members as instruments of unrighteousness unto sin: but yield yourselves unto God, as

those that are alive from the dead, and your members as instruments of righteousness unto God. For sin shall not have dominion over you: for ye are not under the law, but under grace. (Rom. 6:13, 14, KJV)

4. Do you not know that the wicked will not inherit the kingdom of God? Do not be deceived: Neither the sexually immoral nor idolaters nor adulterers nor male prostitutes nor homosexual offenders nor thieves nor the greedy nor drunkards nor slanderers nor swindlers will inherit the kingdom of God. (1 Cor. 6:9, 10, NIV)

5. Flee also youthful lusts: but follow righteousness, faith, charity, peace, with them that call on the Lord out of a pure heart. (2 Tim. 2:22, KJV)

6. And don't forget the cities of Sodom and Gomorrah and their neighboring towns, all full of lust of every kind including lust of men for other men. Those cities were destroyed by fire and continue to be a warning to us that there is a hell in which sinners are punished. (Jude 7, TLB)

For ye have not received the spirit of bondage again to fear; but ye have received the Spirit of adoption, whereby we cry, Abba, Father. (Rom. 8:15, KJV)

Are there any guidelines concerning sexual perversions—"kinky" sex—such as incest,

sodomy, bestiality, sadomasochism?

1. "No one is to approach any close relative to have sexual relations. I am the Lord. Do not dishonor your father by having sexual relations with your mother. She is your mother; do not have relations with her. Do not have sexual relations with your father's wife; that would dishonor your father. Do not have sexual relations with your sister, either your father's daughter or your mother's daughter, whether she was born in the same home or elsewhere. Do not have sexual relations with the daughter of your father's wife, born to your father; she is your sister." (Lev. 18:6-9, 11, NIV)

2. "Do not have sexual relations with an animal and defile yourself with it. A woman must not present herself to an animal to have sexual relations with it; that is a perversion." (Lev. 18:23, NIV)

3. "Cursed is the man who sleeps with his father's wife, for he dishonors his father's bed." Then all the people shall say, "Amen!" "Cursed is the man who has sexual relations with any animal." Then all the people shall say, "Amen!" "Cursed is the man who sleeps with his sister, the daughter of his father or the daughter of his mother." Then all the people shall say, "Amen!" (Deut. 27:20-22, NIV)

4. Do you not know that the unrighteous will not inherit the kingdom of God? Do not be deceived; neither the immoral, nor idolaters, nor adulterers, nor sexual perverts, nor thieves, nor the greedy, nor drunkards, nor revilers, nor robbers will inherit the kingdom of God. (1 Cor. 6:9, 10, RSV)

5. In a similar way, Sodom and Gomorrah and the surrounding towns gave themselves up to sexual immorality and perversion. They serve as an example of those who suffer the punishment of eternal fire. (Jude 7, NIV)

For what the law could not do, in that it was weak through the flesh, God sending his own Son in the likeness of sinful flesh, and for sin, condemned sin in the flesh: that the righteousness of the law might be fulfilled in us, who walk not after the flesh, but after the Spirit. (Rom. 8:3, 4, KJV)

Some people are claiming that extramarital affairs are helpful. Can this be true?

1. "You shall not commit adultery." (Ex. 20:14, NIV)

2. "Do not have intercourse with your neighbor's wife, and defile yourself with her." (Lev. 18:20, NIV)

3. Let thy fountain be blessed: and rejoice with the wife of thy youth. (Prov. 5:18, KJV).

4. But sexual sin is not right: our bodies were not made for that, but for the Lord, and the Lord wants to fill our bodies with himself. . . . Don't you realize that your bodies are actually parts and members of Christ? So should I take part of Christ and join him to a prostitute? Never! (1 Cor. 6:13, 15, TLB)

5. The man should give his wife all that is her right as a

married woman, and the wife should do the same for her husband; for a girl who marries no longer has full right to her own body, for her husband then has his rights to it, too; and in the same way the husband no longer has full right to his own body, for it belongs also to his wife. (1 Cor. 7:3, 4, TLB)

6. Now the works of the flesh are manifest, which are these; Adultery, fornication, uncleanness, lasciviousness . . . envyings, murders, drunkenness, revellings, and such like: of the which I tell you before, as I have also told you in time past, that they which do such things shall not inherit the kingdom of God. (Gal. 5:19, 21, KJV)

7. Honor your marriage and its vows, and be pure; for God will surely punish all those who are immoral or commit adultery. (Heb. 13:4, TLB)

Blessed is the man that endureth temptation: for when he is tried, he shall receive the crown of life, which the Lord hath promised to them that love him. (James 1:12, KJV)

So many people are in an uproar about pornography. Some say it's illegal to stop it because of freedom of the press. Others say it's harmless. Is it really wrong? And if it is, where do I draw the line?

1. "I made a covenant with my eyes not to look with lust upon a girl." (Job 31:1, TLB)

2. I will set no worthless thing before my eyes; I hate the work of those who fall away; It shall not fasten its grip on me. A perverse heart shall depart from me; I will know no evil. (Ps. 101:3, 4, NASB)

3. Turn my eyes away from worthless things; renew my life according to your word. (Ps. 119:37, NIV)

4. "You have heard that it was said, 'You shall not commit adultery'; but I say to you, that every one who looks on a woman to lust for her has committed adultery with her already in his heart." (Matt. 5:27, 28 NASB)

5. "The lamp of your body is your eyes; when your eye is clear, your whole body also is full of light; but when it is bad, your body also is full of darkness." (Luke 11:34, NASB)

6. To set the mind on the flesh is death, but to set the mind on the Spirit is life and peace. (Rom. 8:6, RSV)

7. Finally, brethren, whatever is true, whatever is honorable, whatever is right, whatever is pure, whatever is lovely, whatever is of good repute, if there is any excellence and if anything worthy of praise, let your mind dwell on these things. (Phil. 4:8, NASB)

8. If then you have been raised with Christ, keep seeking the things above, where Christ is, seated at the right hand of God. Set your mind on the things above, not on the things that are on earth. (Col. 3:1, 2, NASB)

9. Therefore consider the members of your earthly body as dead to immorality, impurity, passion, evil desire, and

greed, which amounts to idolatry. For it is on account of these things that the wrath of God will come, and in them you also once walked, when you were living in them. But now you also, put them all aside. (Col. 3:5-8, NASB)

10. And whatever you do, in word or deed, do everything in the name of the Lord Jesus. (Col. 3:17, RSV)

11. Dear brothers, you are only visitors here. Since your real home is in heaven I beg you to keep away from the evil pleasures of this world; they are not for you, for they fight against your very souls. (1 Pet. 2:11, TLB)

Blessed are the pure in heart: for they shall see God. (Matt. 5:8, KJV)

I'm surrounded by sexual temptation—in school, work, books and magazines, TV. How can I cope with it? Can God actually help me to win over temptation?

1. How can a young man stay pure? By reading your Word and following its rules. I have thought much about your words, and stored them in my heart so that they would hold me back from sin. (Ps. 119:9, 11, TLB)

2. Do not offer the parts of your body to sin, as instruments of wickedness, but rather offer yourselves to God, as those who have been brought from death to life; and offer the parts of your body to him as instruments of

righteousness. For sin shall not be your master, because you are not under law, but under grace. (Rom. 6:13, 14, NIV)

3. You have been set free from sin and have become slaves to righteousness. I put this in human terms because you are weak in your natural selves. Just as you used to offer the parts of your body in slavery to impurity and to ever-increasing wickedness, so now offer them in slavery to righteousness leading to holiness. (Rom. 6:18, 19, NIV)

4. Flee from sexual immorality. (1 Cor. 6:18, NIV)

5. But remember this—the wrong desires that come into your life aren't anything new and different. Many others have faced exactly the same problems before you. And no temptation is irresistible. You can trust God to keep the temptation from becoming so strong that you can't stand up against it, for he has promised this and will do what he says. He will show you how to escape temptation's power so that you can bear up patiently against it. (1 Cor. 10:13, TLB)

6. Put to death, therefore, whatever belongs to your earthly nature: Sexual immorality, impurity, lust, evil desires and greed, which is idolatry. But now you must rid yourselves of all such things. (Col. 3:5, 8, NIV)

7. But you, man of God, avoid all these things. Strive for righteousness, godliness, faith, love, endurance, and gentleness. (1 Tim. 6:11, TEV).

8. Flee the evil desires of youth, and pursue righteous-

ness, faith, love and peace, along with those who call on the Lord out of a pure heart. (2 Tim. 2:22, NIV)

9. Because he himself suffered when he was tempted, he is able to help those who are being tempted. (Heb. 2:18, NIV)

10. Turn away from evil and do good. (1 Pet. 3:11, TLB)

11. And so since everything around us is going to melt away, what holy, godly lives we should be living! (2 Pet. 3:11, TLB)

Submit yourselves, then, to God. Resist the devil, and he will flee from you. (James 4:7, NIV)

III. Between Husbands and Wives

It seems that nobody treats others with respect these days. What are God's guidelines for how to treat my spouse?

1. A worthy wife is her husband's joy and crown; the other kind corrodes his strength and tears down everything he does. (Prov. 12:4, TLB)

2. Her children arise and call her blessed; her husband, also, and he praises her: (Prov. 31:28, NIV)

3. Now I want you to realize that the head of every man is Christ, and the head of the woman is man, and the head of Christ is God. (1 Cor. 11:3, NIV)

4. Submit to one another out of reverence for Christ. Wives, submit to your husbands as to the Lord. For the husband is the head of the wife as Christ is the head of the church, his body, of which he is the Savior. Now as the church submits to Christ, so also wives should submit to their husbands in everything. (Eph. 5:21-24, NIV)

5. Husbands, love your wives just as Christ loved the church and gave his life for it. Men ought to love their wives just as they love their own bodies. (Eph. 5:25, 28, TEV)

6. However, each one of you also must love his wife as he loves himself, and the wife must respect her husband. (Eph. 5:33, NIV)

7. Wives, submit to your husbands, as is fitting in the Lord. (Col. 3:18, NIV)

If you can find a truly good wife, she is worth more than precious gems! Her husband can trust her, and she will richly satisfy his needs. (Prov. 31:10, 11, TLB)

Even my close friends are getting divorced. And they have spiritual-sounding reasons for doing it. Are they right?

1. "I hate divorce," says the Lord God of Israel. (Mal. 2:16, NIV)

2. "Haven't you read," he replied, "that at the beginning the Creator 'made them male and female,' and said, 'For this reason a man will leave his father and mother and be united to his wife, and the two will become one flesh'? So they are no longer two, but one. Therefore what God has joined together, let man not separate." (Matt. 19:4-6, NIV)

3. And I say unto you, Whosoever shall put away his wife, except it be for fornication, and shall marry another, committeth adultery: and whoso marrieth her which is put away doth commit adultery. (Matt. 19:9, KJV)

4. He told them, "When a man divorces his wife to marry someone else, he commits adultery against her. And if a wife divorces her husband and remarries, she, too, commits adultery." (Mark 10:11, 12, TLB)

5. "Anyone who divorces his wife and marries another woman commits adultery, and the man who marries a divorced woman commits adultery." (Luke 16:18, NIV)

6. For example, by law a married woman is bound to her husband as long as he is alive, but if her husband dies, she is released from the law of marriage. So then, if she marries another man while her husband is still alive, she is called an adulteress. But if her husband dies, she is released from that law and is not an adulteress, even though she marries another man. (Rom. 7:2, 3, NIV)

7. A wife must not separate from her husband. But if she does, she must remain unmarried or else be reconciled to her husband. And a husband must not divorce his wife. (1 Cor. 7:10, 11, NIV)

8. A woman is bound to her husband as long as he lives. But if her husband dies, she is free to marry anyone she wishes, but he must belong to the Lord. (1 Cor. 7:39, NIV)

I'm a Christian but my spouse is not. How should I treat him/her? What is the best way to win him/her to Christ?

1. Now, for those who are married I have a command, not just a suggestion. And it is not a command from me,

for this is what the Lord himself has said: A wife must not leave her husband. But if she is separated from him, let her remain single or else go back to him. And the husband must not divorce his wife. Here I want to add some suggestions of my own. These are not direct commands from the Lord, but they seem right to me: If a Christian has a wife who is not a Christian, but she wants to stay with him anyway, he must not leave her or divorce her. And if a Christian woman has a husband who isn't a Christian, and he wants her to stay with him, she must not leave him. For perhaps the husband who isn't a Christian may become a Christian with the help of his Christian wife. And the wife who isn't a Christian may become a Christian with the help of her Christian husband. Otherwise, if the family separates, the children might never come to know the Lord; whereas a united family may, in God's plan, result in the children's salvation. But if the husband or wife who isn't a Christian is eager to leave, it is permitted. In such cases the Christian husband or wife should not insist that the other stay, for God wants his children to live in peace and harmony. For, after all, there is no assurance to you wives that your husbands will be converted if they stay; and the same may be said to you husbands concerning your wives. (1 Cor. 7:10-16, TLB)

2. Similarly, you married women, submit to your husbands. Then even if some of them refuse to listen to the Word, you will win them, without talking about it, by the way you wives live, when they see how you fear God and are pure in your lives. (1 Pet. 3:1, 2, Beck)

I can do all things through Christ which strengtheneth me. (Phil. 4:13, KJV)

We're expecting a baby, but we hadn't planned on this one. Maybe an abortion is the answer. What should we do?

1. These are the blessings that will come upon you: blessings in the city, blessings in the field; many children, ample crops; large flocks and herds; blessings of fruit and bread; blessings when you come in, blessings when you go out. (Deut. 28:2-6, TLB)

2. Children are a gift from God; they are his reward. Children born to a young man are like sharp arrows to defend him. Happy is the man who has his quiver full of them. (RSV says sons are a heritage from God.) (Ps. 127:3-5, TLB)

3. May the Lord make you increase, both you and your children. May you be blessed by the Lord, the Maker of heaven and earth. (Ps. 115:14, 15, NIV)

4. Children's children are a crown to the aged. (Prov. 17:6, NIV)

5. Here am I, and the children the Lord has given me. (Isa. 8:18, NIV)

6. But when he seeth his children, the work of mine hands, in the midst of him, they shall sanctify my name. (Isa. 29:23, KJV)

7. "Can a mother forget the baby at her breast, and have no compassion on the child she has borne?" (Isa. 49:15, NIV)

8. Every good and perfect gift is from above, coming down from the Father of the heavenly lights, who does not change like shifting shadows. (James 1:17, NIV)

My spouse and I tend to argue and fight quite often. I know this isn't right, but how can we stop?

1. He puts the righteous and the wicked to the test; he hates those loving violence. He will rain down fire and brimstone on the wicked and scorch them with his burning wind. (Ps. 11:5, TLB)

2. A fool gives full vent to his anger, but a wise man keeps himself under control. (Prov. 29:11, NIV)

3. "Take my yoke upon you and learn from me, for I am gentle and humble in heart, and you will find rest for your souls." (Matt. 11:29, NIV)

4. "But love your enemies, do good to them. . . ." (Luke 6:35, NIV)

5. Be angry but do not sin; do not let the sun go down on your anger. (Eph. 4:26, RSV)

6. Get rid of all bitterness, rage and anger, brawling and slander, along with every form of malice. (Eph. 4:31, NIV)

7. Let your gentleness be evident to all. (Phil. 4:5, NIV)

8. Now the overseer must be above reproach, the husband of but one wife, temperate, self-controlled, respect-

able, hospitable, able to teach, not given to much wine, not violent but gentle, not quarrelsome, not a lover of money. (1 Tim. 3:2, 3, NIV)

Behold, how good and how pleasant it is for breth-ren to dwell together in unity! (Ps. 133:1, KJV)

My spouse has his/her duties and I have mine. I'm busy enough as it is. Should I go out of my way to help him/her?

1. I showed you that it is our duty to help the weak in this way, by hard work. (Acts 20:35, NEB)

2. We who are strong in the faith ought to help the weak to carry their burdens. We should not please ourselves. (Rom. 15:1, TEV)

3. You also must help us by prayer. (2 Cor. 1:11, RSV)

4. Help carry one another's burdens, and in this way you will obey the law of Christ. (Gal. 6:2, TEV)

5. Let us not become weary in doing good, for at the proper time we will reap a harvest if we do not give up. Therefore, as we have opportunity, let us do good to all people, especially to those who belong to the family of believers. (Gal. 6:9, 10, NIV)

6. And we urge you, brothers, warn those who are idle,

encourage the timid, help the weak, be patient with everyone. (1 Thess. 5:14, NIV)

7. In response to all he has done for us, let us outdo each other in being helpful and kind to each other and in doing good. (Heb. 10:24, TLB)

8. So we say with confidence, "The Lord is my helper." (Heb. 13:6, NIV)

Extramarital affairs are almost stylish today. Is it worth the effort to remain faithful?

1. Your wife will be like a fruitful vine within your house; your sons will be like olive shoots around your table. Thus is the man blessed who fears the Lord. (Ps. 128:3, 4, NIV)

2. Rejoice in the wife of your youth. Let her charms and tender embrace satisfy you. Let her love alone fill you with delight. (Prov. 5:18, 19, TLB)

3. Live happily with the woman you love through the fleeting days of life, for the wife God gives you is your best reward down here for all your earthly toil. (Eccles. 9:9, TLB)

4. "So they are no longer two, but one." (Matt. 19:6, NIV)

5. Let marriage be held in honor among all, and let the marriage bed be undefiled; for God will judge the immoral and adulterous. (Heb. 13:4, RSV)

IV. Between Parents and Children

It seems some kid at school or on the block is always looking for a fight. And my child seems happy to oblige. What can I tell him/her that will prevent the fighting?

1. The beginning of strife is like letting out water; so quit before the quarrel breaks out. (Prov. 17:14, RSV)

2. Keeping away from strife is an honor for a man, But any fool will quarrel. (Prov. 20:3, NASB)

3. "Blessed are the peacemakers, for they shall be called the sons of God." (Matt. 5:9, RSV)

4. "But I have added to that rule, and tell you that if you are only angry, even in your own home, you are in danger of judgment! If you call your friend an idiot, you are in danger of being brought before the court. And if you curse him, you are in danger of the fires of hell." (Matt. 5:22, TLB)

5. "A new commandment I give to you, that you love one another; even as I have loved you, that you also love one another. By this all men will know that you are my disciples, if you have love for one another." (John 13:34, 35, RSV)

6. Hold them in the highest regard in love because of their work. Live in peace with each other. (1 Thess. 5:13, NIV)

7. Pursue peace with all men, and the sanctification without which no one will see the Lord. (Heb. 12:14, NASB)

My child is making a habit of lying or exaggerating. What can I say to him/her in order to stop the practice?

1. "Do not lie. Do not deceive one another." (Lev. 19:11, NIV)

2. Keep your tongue from evil and your lips from speaking lies. (Ps. 34:13, NIV)

3. Surely you desire truth in the inner parts; you teach me wisdom in the inmost place. (Ps. 51:6, NIV)

4. For there are six things the Lord hates—no, seven: Haughtiness, Lying. . . . (Prov. 6:16, 17, TLB)

5. The Lord detests lying lips, but he delights in men who are truthful. (Prov. 12:22, NIV)

6. "Speak the truth to each other, and render true and sound judgment in your courts." (Zech. 8:16, NIV)

7. "You belong to your father, the devil, and you want to carry out your father's desire. He was a murderer from the beginning, not holding to the truth, for there is no

truth in him. When he lies, he speaks his native language, for he is a liar and the father of lies." (John 8:44, NIV)

8. No more lying, then! Everyone must tell the truth to his fellow believer, Because we are all members together in the body of Christ. (Eph. 4:25, TEV)

9. Do not lie to one another, for you have put off the old self with its habits. (Col. 3:9, TEV)

10. But the cowardly, the unbelieving, the vile, the murderers, the sexually immoral, those who practice magic acts, the idolaters and all liars—their place will be in the fiery lake of burning sulfur. This is the second death. (Rev. 21:8, NIV)

For my mouth shall speak truth; and wickedness is an abomination to my lips. (Prov. 8:7, KJV)

My child's friends are growing weary of his/her bragging. I know boasting is wrong, but how can I convince my child to stop doing it?

1. May the Lord cut off all flattering lips and every boastful tongue. (Ps. 12:3, NIV)

2. Glorify your name, not ours, O Lord! (Ps. 115:1, TLB)

3. Don't praise yourself; let others do it! (Prov. 27:2, TLB)

4. This is what the Lord says: "Let not the wise man boast of his wisdom or the strong man boast of his strength or the rich man boast of his riches, but let him who boasts boast about this: that he understands and knows me." (Jer. 9:23, 24, NIV)

5. Your boasting is not good. (1 Cor. 5:6, NIV)

I have discovered that my child is earning a reputation as a gossip. How can I put an end to this behavior?

1. For there are six things the Lord hates—no, seven: . . . a false witness, sowing discord among brothers. (Prov. 6:16, 19, TLB)

2. An evil man sows strife; gossip separates the best of friends. (Prov. 16:28, TLB)

3. Don't tell your secrets to a gossip unless you want them broadcast to the world. (Prov. 20:19, TLB)

4. Furthermore, since they did not think it worthwhile to retain the knowledge of God, he gave them over to a depraved mind, to do what ought not to be done. They have become filled with every kind of wickedness, evil, greed and depravity. They are full of envy, murder, strife, deceit and malice. They are gossips. . . . Although they know God's righteous decree that those who do such things deserve death, they not only continue to do these very things but also approve of those who practice them. (Rom. 1:28, 29, 32, NIV)

5. Have nothing to do with godless myths and old wives' tales; rather, train yourself to be godly. (1 Tim. 4:7, NIV)

6. Don't have anything to do with foolish and stupid arguments, because you know they produce quarrels. (2 Tim. 2:23, NIV)

7. Don't criticize and speak evil about each other, dear brothers. (James 4:11, TLB)

Pleasant words are as an honeycomb, sweet to the soul, and health to the bones. (Prov. 16:24, KJV)

The words my child picks up at school and play horrify me. I realize he/she can't help hearing them, but how can I prevent those words from being used in my family?

1. "You shall not misuse the name of the Lord your God, for the Lord will not hold anyone guiltless who misuses his name." (Ex. 20:7, NIV)

2. Don't use bad language. Say only what is good and helpful to those you are talking to, and what will give them a blessing. (Eph. 4:29, TLB)

3. Get rid of all bitterness, passion, and anger. No more shouting or insults, no more hateful feelings of any sort. (Eph. 4:31, TEV)

4. Let no one be able to accuse you of any such things.

Dirty stories, foul talk and coarse jokes—these are not for you. Instead, remind each other of God's goodness and be thankful. (Eph. 5:3, 4, TLB)

5. But now you must get rid of all these things: anger, passion, and hateful feelings. No insults or obscene talk must ever come from your lips. (Col. 3:8, TEV)

6. We use [our tongues] to give thanks to our Lord and Father and also to curse our fellow-man who is created in the likeness of God. Words of thanksgiving and cursing pour out from the same mouth. My brothers, this should not happen! (James 3:9, 10, TEV)

And whatever you do, in word or deed, do everything in the name of the Lord Jesus, giving thanks to God the Father through him. (Col. 3:17, RSV)

My child is no longer satisfied with the things he/she has. The old "when I was your age" argument won't work. What will?

1. Better a little with righteousness than much gain with injustice. (Prov. 16:8, NIV)

2. "And be content with your wages." (Luke 3:14, KJV)

3. I am not saying this because I am in need, for I have learned to be content whatever the circumstances. I know what it is to be in need, and I know what it is to have

plenty. I have learned the secret of being content in any and every situation, whether well fed or hungry, whether living in plenty or in want. I can do everything through him who gives me strength. (Phil. 4:11-13, NIV)

4. But godliness with contentment is great gain. (1 Tim. 6:6, NIV)

5. Keep your lives free from the love of money and be content with what you have, because God has said, "Never will I leave you; never will I forsake you." (Heb. 13:5, NIV)

My child doesn't believe God can and will provide his/her genuine needs. What should I tell him/her?

1. The Lord is my Shepherd, I shall lack nothing. (Ps. 23:1, NIV)

2. The young lions suffer want and hunger; but those who seek the Lord lack no good thing. (Ps. 34:10, RSV)

3. "So do not start worrying: 'Where will my food come from? or my drink? or my clothes?' (These are the things the pagans are always concerned about.) Your Father in heaven knows that you need all these things. Instead, be concerned above anything else with the Kingdom of God and with what he requires of you, and he will provide you with all these other things." (Matt. 6:31-33, TEV)

4. And God is able to give you more than you need, so

that you will always have all you need for yourselves and more than enough for every good cause. (2 Cor. 9:8, TEV)

5. But my God shall supply all your need according to his riches in glory by Christ Jesus. (Phil. 4:19, KJV)

My child tells me that his/her friends often steal when they want something. I'm afraid he/she is losing sight of the sinfulness of stealing. What should I say to bolster his/her conscience?

1. "You shall not steal." (Ex. 20:15, NIV)

2. "Do not steal." (Lev. 19:11, NIV)

3. "Do not defraud your neighbor or rob him." (Lev. 19:13, NIV)

4. Do you not know that the wicked will not inherit the kingdom of God? Do not be deceived: Neither the sexually immoral . . . nor thieves . . . will inherit the kingdom of God. (1 Cor. 6:9, 10, NIV)

But seek ye first the kingdom of God, and his righteousness; and all these things shall be added unto you. (Matt. 6:33, KJV)

I have discovered that my child has shoplifted some items. What should I say as I confront him/her?

1. "A thief must certainly make restitution, but if he has nothing, he must be sold to pay for his theft." (Ex. 22:3, NIV)

2. "When he thus sins and becomes guilty, he must return what he has stolen or taken by extortion, or what was entrusted to him, or the lost property he found, or whatever it was he swore falsely about. He must make restitution in full, add a fifth of the value to it and give it all to the owner on the day he presents his guilt offering." (Lev. 6:4, 5, NIV)

3. Let the thief no longer steal, but rather let him labor, doing honest work with his hands, so that he may be able to give to those in need. (Eph. 4:28, RSV)

Sometimes when I punish my child for disobedience, I feel as if I'm doing the wrong thing. What is the proper way to discipline?

1. Do not withhold discipline from a child; if you punish him with the rod, he will not die. Punish him with the rod and save his soul from death. (Prov. 23:13, 14, NIV)

2. The rod of correction imparts wisdom, but a child left to itself disgraces his mother. (Prov. 29:15, NIV)

3. Discipline your son, and he will give you peace; he will

bring delight to your soul. (Prov. 29:17, NIV)

4. Fathers, do not exasperate your children; instead, bring them up in the training and instruction of the Lord. (Eph. 6:4, NIV)

5. Fathers, don't scold your children so much that they become discouraged and quit trying. (Col. 3:21, TLB)

6. And have you forgotten the exhortation which addresses you as sons?—"My son, do not regard lightly the discipline of the Lord, nor lose courage when you are punished by him. For the Lord disciplines him whom he loves, and chastises every son whom he receives. (Heb. 12:5, 6, RSV)

7. No discipline seems pleasant at the time, but painful. Later on, however, it produces a harvest of righteousness and peace for those who have been trained by it. (Heb. 12:11, NIV)

I see so much disrespect toward parents and I don't want my child to develop that kind of attitude. How can I insure that he/ she will not display such behavior?

1. "Honor your father and mother, that you may have a long, good life in the land the Lord your God will give you." (Ex. 20:12, TLB)

2. Then he went down to Nazareth with them and was obedient to them. But his mother treasured all these

things in her heart. (Luke 2:51, 52, NIV)

3. Children, obey your parents; this is the right thing to do because God has placed them in authority over you. (Eph. 6:1, TLB)

4. Children, obey your parents in everything, for this pleases the Lord. (Col. 3:20, NIV)

5. But if a widow has children or grandchildren, these should learn first of all to put their religion into practice by caring for their own family and so repaying their parents and grandparents, for this is pleasing to God. (1 Tim. 5:4, NIV)

Even I, as an adult, have trouble understanding the Bible. Does it do any good to teach and read the Bible to my child while he/she is so young?

1. These commandments that I give you today are to be upon your hearts. Impress them on your children. Talk about them when you sit at home and when you walk along the road, when you lie down and when you get up. (Deut. 6:6, 7, NIV)

2. "Call them all together," the Lord instructed, "—men, women, children, and foreigners living among you—to hear the laws of God and to learn his will, so that you will reverence the Lord your God and obey his laws. Do this so that your little children who have not known these laws will hear them and learn how to revere the Lord your

God as long as you live in the Promised Land." (Deut. 31:12, 13, TLB)

3. Train a child in the way he should go, and when he is old he will not turn from it. (Prov. 22:6, NIV)

4. When Jesus saw this, he was indignant. He said to them, "Let the little children come to me, and do not hinder them, for the kingdom of God belongs to such as these." (Mark 10:14, NIV)

5. You know how, when you were a small child, you were taught the holy Scriptures; and it is these that make you wise to accept God's salvation by trusting in Christ Jesus. (2 Tim. 3:15, TLB)

V. Health and Outward Appearance

Some people say makeup, jewelry and concern with personal appearance is vanity and even sinful. What is right? What are God's guidelines?

1. A woman must not wear men's clothing, nor a man wear women's clothing, for the Lord your God detests anyone who does this. (Deut. 22:5, NIV)

2. "Since you have forgotten me and thrust me behind your back, you must bear the consequences of your lewdness and prostitution. They even sent messengers for men who came from far away, and when they arrived you bathed yourself for them, painted your eyes and put on your jewelry." (Ezek. 23:35, 40, NIV)

3. And whatever you do, in word or deed, do everything in the name of the Lord Jesus. (Col. 3:17, RSV)

4. I also want the women to be modest and sensible about their clothes and to dress properly; not with fancy hair styles or with gold ornaments or pearls or expensive dresses, but with good deeds, as is proper for women who claim to be religious. (1 Tim. 2:9, 10, TEV)

5. Don't be concerned about the outward beauty that

depends on jewelry, or beautiful clothes, or hair arrangement. Be beautiful inside, in your hearts, with the lasting charm of a gentle and quiet spirit which is so precious to God. (1 Peter 3:3, 4, TLB)

I feel that God has cheated me by not giving me a more attractive body. How am I supposed to feel about this?

1. But the Lord said to Samuel, "Don't judge by a man's face or height, for this is not the one. I don't make decisions the way you do! Men judge by outward appearance, but I look at a man's thoughts and intentions. (1 Sam. 16:7, TLB)

2. Thou it was who didst fashion my inward parts; thou didst knit me together in my mother's womb. I will praise thee, for thou dost fill me with awe; wonderful thou art, and wonderful thy works. Thou knowest me through and through: my body is no mystery to thee, how I was secretly kneaded into shape and patterned in the depths of the earth. Thou didst see my limbs unformed in the womb, and in thy book they are all recorded. (Ps. 139:13-16, NEB)

3. A happy heart makes the face cheerful. (Prov. 15:13, NIV)

4. Charm is deceptive, and beauty is fleeting; but a woman who fears the Lord is to be praised. (Prov. 31:30, NIV)

5. [Jesus] had no beauty or majesty to attract us to him,

nothing in his appearance that we should desire him. (Isa. 53:2, NIV)

6. The Lord their God will save them on that day as the flock of his people. They will sparkle in his land like jewels in a crown. How attractive and beautiful they will be! (Zech. 9:16, 17, NIV)

7. But who are you, O man, to talk back to God? "Shall what is formed say to him who formed it, 'Why did you make me like this?' " (Rom. 9:20, NIV)

8. Don't be concerned about the outward beauty that depends on jewelry, or beautiful clothes, or hair arrangement. Be beautiful inside, in your hearts, with the lasting charm of a gentle and quiet spirit which is so precious to God. (1 Pet. 3:3, 4, TLB)

I'm confused by all the fad diets, the health-food addicts and the people who don't care what they eat. What is the right attitude toward food?

1. For the drunkard and the glutton will come to poverty. (Prov. 23:21, RSV)

2. At the end of ten days it was seen that they were better in appearance and fatter in flesh than all the youths who ate the king's rich food. So the steward took away their rich food and the wine they were to drink, and gave them vegetables. (Dan. 1:15, 16, RSV)

3. Blessed are they which do hunger and thirst after righteousness: for they shall be filled. (Matt. 5:6, KJV)

4. Therefore take no thought, saying, What shall we eat? or, What shall we drink? or, Wherewithal shall we be clothed? (For after all these things do the Gentiles seek:) for your heavenly Father knoweth that ye have need of all these things. But seek ye first the kingdom of God, and his righteousness; and all these things shall be added unto you. (Matt. 6:31-33, KJV)

5. He who eats meat, eats to the Lord, for he gives thanks to God; and he who abstains, does so to the Lord and gives thanks to God. (Rom 14:6, NIV)

6. All things are lawful unto me, but all things are not expedient: all things are lawful for me, but I will not be brought under the power of any. (1 Cor. 6:12, KJV)

7. You are not your own, you were bought at a price; Therefore honor God with your body. (1 Cor. 6:19, 20, NIV)

8. But food does not bring us near to God. (1 Cor. 8:8, NIV)

9. So whether you eat or drink or whatever you do, do it all for the glory of God. (1 Cor. 10:31, NIV)

10. For many walk, of whom I have told you often, and now tell you even weeping, that they are the enemies of the cross of Christ: whose end is destruction, whose God is their belly, and whose glory is in their shame, who mind earthly things. (Phil. 3:18, 19, KJV)

For the kingdom of God is not meat and drink; but righteousness, and peace, and joy in the Holy Ghost. (Rom. 14:17, KJV)

We live in such a casual, even crass, society that I'm sometimes embarrassed to use proper manners. How much is enough?

1. He suddenly noticed three men coming toward him. He sprang up and ran to meet them and welcomed them. "Sirs," he said, "please don't go any further. Stop awhile and rest here in the shade of this tree while I get water to refresh your feet, and a bite to eat to strengthen you. Do stay awhile before continuing your journey." "All right," they said, "do as you have said." Then Abraham ran back to the tent and said to Sarah, "Quick! Mix up some pancakes! Use your best flour, and make enough for the three of them!" Then he ran out to the herd and selected a fat calf and told a servant to hurry and butcher it. Soon, taking them cheese and milk and the roast veal, he set it before the men and stood beneath the trees beside them as they ate. (Abraham showed politeness and hospitality.) (Gen. 18:2-8, TLB)

2. All the royal officials at the king's gate knelt down and paid honor to Haman, for the king had commanded this concerning him. But Mordecai would not kneel down or pay him honor. Haman went out that day happy and in high spirits. But when he saw Mordecai at the king's gate and observed that he neither rose nor showed fear in his presence, he was filled with rage against Mordecai.

(Mordecai realized that devotion to God sometimes supersedes "good manners.") (Esther 3:2; 5:9, NIV)

3. When he saw Queen Esther standing in the court, he was pleased with her and held out to her the gold scepter that was in his hand. So Esther approached and touched the tip of the scepter. (Esther followed accepted custom as she approach the king, her husband.) (Esther 5:2, NIV)

4. Then Peter, filled with the Holy Spirit, said to them, "Honorable leaders and elders of our nations, if you mean the good deed done to the cripple, and how he was healed. . . ." (Peter addressed even his leaders politely.) (Acts 4:8-10, TLB)

5. King Agrippa, I consider myself fortunate to stand before you today as I make my defense against all the accusations of the Jews, and especially so because you are well acquainted with all the Jewish customs and controversies. Therefore, I beg you to listen to me patiently. (Paul addressed dignitaries politely.) (Acts 26:2, 3, NIV)

Is proper and polite speech just vain effort or does God actually care about the way I talk to people?

1. A man finds joy in giving an apt reply—and how good is a timely word! (Prov. 15:23, NIV)

2. A word aptly spoken is like apples of gold in settings of silver. (Prov. 25:11, NIV)

3. Don't use bad language. Say only what is good and helpful to those you are talking to, and what will give them a blessing. (Eph. 4:29, TLB)

4. Talk with each other much about the Lord, quoting psalms and hymns and singing sacred songs, making music in your hearts to the Lord. Always give thanks for everything to our God and Father in the name of our Lord Jesus Christ. (Eph. 5:19, 20, TLB)

5. And whatever you do, in word or deed, do everything in the name of the Lord Jesus, giving thanks to God the Father through him. (Col. 3:17, RSV)

6. Let your conversation be gracious as well as sensible, for then you will have the right answer for everyone. (Col. 4:6, TLB)

7. Do not pay back evil with evil or cursing with cursing; instead, pay back with a blessing, because a blessing is what God promised to give you when he called you. As the scripture says, "Whoever wants to enjoy life and wishes to see good times, must keep from speaking evil and stop telling lies." (1 Pet. 3:9, 10, TEV)

Being a Christian doesn't seem to make me immune to sickness. How should I view health problems?

1. "For I am the Lord who heals you." (Ex. 15:26, NIV)

2. Yes, I will bless the Lord and not forget the glorious

things he does for me. He forgives all my sins. He heals me. (Ps. 103:2, 3, TLB)

3. Fear the Lord and shun evil. This will bring health to your body and nourishment to your bones. (Prov. 3:7, 8, NIV)

4. This fulfilled the prophecy of Isaiah, "He took our sick-nesses and bore our diseases." (Matt. 8:17, TLB)

5. Is any one of you sick? He should call the elders of the church to pray over him and anoint him with oil in the name of the Lord. And the prayer offered in faith will make the sick person well; the Lord will raise him up. If he has sinned, he will be forgiven. Therefore confess your sins to each other and pray for each other so that you may be healed. (James 5:14-16, NIV)

VI. Entertainment and Social Life

Parents and kids can never seem to agree on what music to listen to. How can our family discuss and judge music?

1. May they sing of the ways of the Lord, for the glory of the Lord is great. (Ps. 138:5, NIV)

2. Praise the Lord! For it is good to sing praises to our God; for he is gracious, and a song of praise is seemly. (Ps. 147:1, RSV)

3. Sing to the Lord with thanksgiving; make music to our God on the harp. (Ps. 147:7, NIV)

4. Speak to one another in psalms, hymns, and songs; sing and make music in your hearts to the Lord. (Eph. 5:19, NEB)

5. Whatever is pure ... think about such things. (Phil. 4:8, NIV)

6. Sing thankfully in your hearts to God, with psalms and hymns and spiritual songs ... in the name of the Lord Jesus. (Col. 3:16, 17, NEB)

7. And whatever you do, in word or deed, do everything in the name of the Lord Jesus. (Col. 3:17, RSV)

I'd like to date a person who's not a true Christian. Some of my friends tell me it would be a great chance for witnessing. But my parents and pastor disagree. Who's right?

1. I am a friend to all who fear you, to all who follow your precepts. (Ps. 119:63, NIV)

2. Can two walk together, except they be agreed? (Amos 3:3, KJV)

3. "Everything is permissible for me"—but not everything is beneficial. "Everything is permissible for me"—but I will not be mastered by anything. (1 Cor. 6:12, NIV)

4. Do not be misled: "Bad company corrupts good character." (1 Cor. 15:33, NIV)

5. Do not be mismated with unbelievers. For what partnership have righteousness and iniquity? Or what fellowship has light with darkness? (2 Cor. 6:14, RSV)

6. How can Christ and the Devil agree? What does a believer have in common with an unbeliever? How can God's temple come to terms with pagan idols? For we are the temple of the living God! As God himself has said, "I will make my home with my people and live among them, I will be their God, and they shall be my people." And so the Lord says, "You must leave them, and separate yourselves from them. Have nothing to do with what is unclean, and I will accept you. I will be your father, and you shall be my sons and daughters, says the

Lord Almighty." All these promises are made to us, my dear friends. So then, let us purify ourselves from everything that makes body or soul unclean, and let us be completely holy by living in reverence for God. (2 Cor. 6:15-7:1, TEV)

7. Therefore do not associate with them, for once you were darkness, but now you are light in the Lord; walk as children of light. (Eph. 5:7, 8, RSV)

8. Unfaithful people! Don't you know that to be the world's friend means to be God's enemy? Whoever wants to be the world's friend makes himself God's enemy. (James 4:44, TEV)

9. But you are not like that, for you have been chosen by God himself—you are priests of the King; you are holy and pure, you are God's very own—all this so that you may show to others how God called you out of darkness into his wonderful light. (1 Pet. 2:9, TLB)

It's hard to be a Christian when it seems everyone else isn't. I need some friends. Can I have some who aren't Christians?

1. "Do not follow the crowd in doing wrong." (Ex. 23:2, NIV)

2. If young toughs tell you, "Come and join us"—turn your back on them! (Prov. 1:10, TLB)

3. He who walks with wise men becomes wise, but the companion of fools will suffer harm. (Prov. 13:20, RSV)

4. Don't let the world around you squeeze you into its own mold, but let God remold your minds from within, so that you may prove in practice that the plan of God for you is good, meets all his demands and moves toward the goal of true maturity. (Rom. 12:2, Phillips)

5. Do not be misled: "Bad company corrupts good character." (1 Cor. 15:33, NIV)

6. Do not try to work together as equals with unbelievers, for it cannot be done. How can right and wrong be partners? How can light and darkness live together? How can Christ and the Devil agree? What does a believer have in common with an unbeliever? (2 Cor. 6:14, 15, TEV)

7. Unfaithful people! Don't you know that to be the world's friend means to be God's enemy? Whoever wants to be the world's friend makes himself God's enemy. (James 4:4, TEV)

TV offers many bad programs, but also many good ones. How can I decide what I should watch?

1. I will set before my eyes no vile thing. (Ps. 101:3, NIV)

2. Turn my eyes away from worthless things. (Ps. 119:37, NIV)

3. I can do anything I want to if Christ has not said no, but some of these things aren't good for me. Even if I am allowed to do them, I'll refuse to if I think they might get

such a grip on me that I can't easily stop when I want to. (1 Cor. 6:12, TLB)

4. For you were once darkness, but now you are light in the Lord. Live as children of light (for the fruit of the light consists in all goodness, righteousness and truth) and find out what pleases the Lord. Have nothing to do with the fruitless deeds of darkness. (Eph. 5:8-11, NIV)

5. Live life, then, with a due sense of responsibility, not as men who do not know the meaning and purpose of life but as those who do. Make the best use of your time, despite all the difficulties of these days. (Eph. 5:15, 16, Phillips)

6. Finally brothers, whatever is true, whatever is noble, whatever is right, whatever is pure, whatever is lovely, whatever is admirable—if anything is excellent or praiseworthy—think about such things. (Phil. 4:8, NIV)

7. And whatever you do, in word or deed, do everything in the name of the Lord Jesus. (Col. 3:17, RSV)

8. You will never be able to eat solid spiritual food and understand the deeper things of God's word until you become better Christians and learn right from wrong by practicing doing right. (Heb. 5:14, TLB)

9. Therefore, since we are surrounded by such a great cloud of witnesses, let us throw off everything that hinders and the sin that so easily entangles, and let us run with perseverance the race marked out for us. Let us fix our eyes on Jesus. (Heb. 12:1, 2, NIV)

10. But these very teachers who offer this "freedom" from law are themselves slaves to sin and destruction. For a man is a slave to whatever controls him. (2 Pet. 2:19, TLB)

VII. Christian Life

So often we have little or no time to pray to-gether and seemingly no time to pray alone. How conscientious should we be?

1. As for me, far be it from me that I should sin against the Lord by failing to pray for you. And I will teach you the way that is good and right. (1 Sam. 12:23, NIV)

2. "When you pray, do not be like the hypocrites! They love to stand up and pray in the houses of worship and on the street corners so that everyone will see them. I assure you, they have already been paid in full. But when you pray, go to your room, close the door, and pray to your Father, who is unseen. And your Father, who sees what you do in private, will reward you." (Matt. 6:5, 6, TEV)

3. "Watch and pray so that you will not fall into temptation. The spirit is willing, but the body is weak." (Mark 14:38, NIV)

4. And he said to them, "The harvest is plentiful, but the laborers are few; pray therefore the Lord of the harvest to send out laborers into his harvest." (Luke 10:2, RSV)

5. Then Jesus told the disciples a parable to show them

that they should always pray and not give up. (Luke 18:1, NIV)

6. And in the same way—by our faith—the Holy Spirit helps us with our daily problems and in our praying. For we don't even know what we should pray for, nor how to pray as we should; but the Holy Spirit prays for us with such feeling that it cannot be expressed in words. (Rom. 8:26, TLB)

7. Give yourselves wholly to prayer and entreaty; pray on every occasion in the power of the Spirit. To this end keep watch and persevere, always interceding for all God's people. (Eph. 6:18, NEB)

8. Pray continually. (1 Thess. 5:17, NIV)

9. First of all, then, I urge that petitions, prayers, requests, and thanksgivings be offered to God for all people. (1 Tim. 2:1, TEV)

10. The prayer of a righteous man is powerful and effective. (James 5:16, NIV)

11. But you, my friends, keep on building yourselves up on your most sacred faith. Pray in the power of the Holy Spirit. (Jude 20, TEV)

And this is the confidence that we have in him, that, if we ask anything according to his will, he heareth us: and if we know that he hear us, whatsoever we ask, we know that we have the petitions that we desired of him. (1 John 5:14, 15, KJV)

So many claim there is no God—and some days I feel it might be true! How can I reassure myself that He lives and listens to me?

1. But ask the animals, and they will teach you, or the birds of the air, and they will tell you. Which of all these does not know that the hand of the Lord has done this? (Job 12:7, 9, NIV)

2. In his pride the wicked does not seek him; in all his thoughts there is no room for God. (Ps. 10:4, NIV)

3. The fool says in his heart, "There is no God." (Ps. 14:1, NIV)

4. The Heavens are telling the glory of God; they are a marvelous display of his craftsmanship. Day and night they keep on telling about God. (Ps. 19:1, 2, TLB)

5. "God is Spirit, and those who worship him must worship in spirit and truth." (John 4:24, RSV)

6. "He created all the people of the world from one man, Adam, and scattered the nations across the face of the earth. He decided beforehand which should rise and fall, and when. He determined their boundaries. His purpose in all of this is that they should seek after God, and perhaps feel their way toward him and find him—though he is not far from any one of us." (Acts 17:26, 27, TLB)

7. God punishes them, because what can be known about God is plain to them, for God himself made it plain to them. Ever since God created the world, his invisible qualities, both his eternal power and his divine nature,

have been clearly seen; They are perceived in the things that God has made. So those people have no excuse at all. (Rom. 1:19, 20, TEV)

8. And without faith it is impossible to please him. For whoever would draw near to God must believe that he exists and that he rewards those who seek him. (Heb. 11:6, RSV)

My friends are calling me names because I stand up for what the Bible says. It's hard not to get bitter. How am I supposed to feel about this?

1. "If the world hates you, keep in mind that it hated me first. If you belonged to the world, it would love you as its own. As it is, you do not belong to the world, but I have chosen you out of the world. That is why the world hates you." (John 15:18, 19, NIV)

2. "I have said this to you, that in me you may have peace. In the world you have tribulation; but be of good cheer, I have overcome the world." (John 16:33, RSV)

3. Who, then, can separate us from the love of Christ? Can trouble do it, or hardship or persecution or hunger or poverty or danger or death? For I am certain that nothing can separate us from his love; neither death nor life, neither angels nor other heavenly rulers or powers, neither the present nor the future, neither the world above nor the world below—there is nothing in all creation that will ever be able to separate us from the love of

God which is ours through Christ Jesus our Lord. (Rom. 8:35, 38, 39, TEV)

4. You can be sure that the more we undergo sufferings for Christ, the more he will shower us with his comfort and encouragement. (2 Cor. 1:5, TLB)

5. And if we think that our present service for him is hard, just remember that some day we are going to sit with him and rule with him. But if we give up when we suffer, and turn against Christ, then he must turn against us. (2 Tim. 2:12, TLB)

6. In fact, everyone who wants to live a godly life in Christ Jesus will be persecuted. (2 Tim. 3:12, NIV)

7. Let us fix our eyes on Jesus, the author and perfector of our faith, who for the joy set before him endured the cross, scorning its shame, and sat down at the right hand of the throne of God. Consider him who endured such opposition from sinful men, so that you will not grow weary and lose heart. In your struggle against sin, you have not yet resisted to the point of shedding your blood. (Heb. 12:2-4, NIV)

8. But even if you do suffer for righteousness' sake, you will be blessed. Have no fear of them, nor be troubled, but in your hearts reverence Christ as Lord. Always be prepared to make a defense to any one who calls you to account for the hope that is in you, yet do it with gentleness and reverence; and keep your conscience clear, so that, when you are abused, those who revile your good behavior in Christ may be put to shame. (1 Pet. 3:14-16, RSV)

9. Dear friends, do not be surprised at the painful trial you are suffering, as though something strange were happening to you. But rejoice that you participate in the sufferings of Christ, so that you may be overjoyed when his glory is revealed. (1 Pet. 4:12, 13, NIV)

I feel that I'm a failure in everything I do. Does God really love me? Can He possibly use me?

1. "For I am the Lord, your God, who takes hold of your right hand and says to you, Do not fear; I will help you." (Isa. 41:13, NIV)

2. "But when they arrest you, do not worry about what to say or how to say it. At that time you will be given what to say, for it will not be you speaking, but the Spirit of your Father speaking through you." (Matt. 10:19, 20, NIV)

3. "Remain in me, and I will remain in you. No branch can bear fruit by itself; it must remain in the vine. Neither can you bear fruit unless you remain in me. I am the vine; you are the branches. If a man remains in me and I in him, he will bear much fruit; apart from me you can do nothing." (John 15:4, 5, NIV)

4. "You did not choose me, but I chose you and appointed you." (John 15:16, RSV)

5. Brothers, think of what you were when you were called. Not many of you were wise by human standards; not many were influential; not many were of noble birth.

But God chose the foolish things of the world to shame the wise; God chose the weak things of the world to shame the strong. He chose the lowly things of this world and the despised things—and the things that are not—to nullify the things that are, so that no one may boast before him. It is because of him that you are in Christ Jesus, who has become for us wisdom from God—that is, our righteousness, holiness and redemption. Therefore, as it is written: "Let him who boasts boast in the Lord." (1 Cor. 1:26-31, NIV)

6. But we have this treasure in jars of clay to show that this all-surpassing power is from God and not from us. (2 Cor. 4:7, NIV)

7. Each time he said, "No. But I am with you; that is all you need. My power shows up best in weak people." Now I am glad to boast about how weak I am; I am glad to be a living demonstration of Christ's power, instead of showing off my own power and abilities. (2 Cor. 12:9, TLB)

8. Last of all I want to remind you that your strength must come from the Lord's mighty power within you. (Eph. 6:10, TLB)

9. For I can do everything God asks me to with the help of Christ who gives me the strength and power. (Phil. 4:13, TLB)

Fear thou not; for I am with thee: be not dismayed; for I am thy God: I will strengthen thee; yea, I will help thee; yea, I will uphold thee with the right hand of my righteousness. (Isa. 41:10, KJV)

It seems unfair that I should have to work when I could be having fun. Shouldn't enjoyment be more important than work?

1. Six days you shall labor and do all your work. (Ex. 20:9, NIV)

2. Take a lesson from the ants, you lazy fellow. Learn from their ways and be wise! For though they have no king to make them work, yet they labor hard all summer, gathering food for the winter. But you—all you do is sleep. When will you wake up? "Let me sleep a little longer!" Sure, just a little more! And as you sleep, poverty creeps upon you like a robber and destroys you; want attacks you in full armor. (Prov. 6:6-11, TLB)

3. Laziness brings on deep sleep, and the shiftless man goes hungry. (Prov. 19:15, NIV)

4. The lazy man won't go out and work. . . . Yet in his own opinion he is smarter than seven wise men. (Prov. 26:13, 16, TLB)

5. Never be lazy in your work but serve the Lord enthusiastically. (Rom. 12:11, TLB)

6. Work hard and cheerfully at all you do, just as though you were working for the Lord and not merely for your masters, remembering that it is the Lord Christ who is going to pay you, giving you your full portion of all he owns. He is the one you are really working for. And if you don't do your best for him, he will pay you in a way that you won't like—for he has no special favorites who can get away with shirking. (Col. 3:23-25, TLB)

7. Surely you remember, brothers, our toil and hardship; we worked night and day in order not to be a burden to anyone while we preached the gospel of God to you. (1 Thess. 2:9, NIV)

8. Make it your ambition to lead a quiet life, to mind your own business and to work with your hands, just as we told you, so that your daily life may win the respect of outsiders and so that you will not be dependent on anybody. (1 Thess. 4:11, 12, NIV)

9. Dear brothers, warn those who are lazy. (1 Thess. 5:14, TLB)

10. Our brothers, we command you in the name of the Lord Jesus Christ to keep away from all brothers who are living a lazy life and who do not follow the instructions that we gave them. You yourselves know very well that you should do just what we did. We were not lazy when we were with you. We did not accept anyone's support without paying for it. Instead, we worked and toiled; We kept working day and night so as not to be an expense to any of you. While we were with you, we told you,— "Whoever refuses to work is not allowed to eat." (2 Thess. 3:6-8, 10, TEV)

Yet we hear that some of you are living in laziness, refusing to work, and wasting your time in gossiping. In the name of the Lord Jesus Christ we appeal to such people—we command them—to quiet down, get to work, and earn their own living. (2 Thess. 3:11, 12, TLB)

Should I really care what happens to other people? Should I be as concerned with their success as with my own?

1. "But love your neighbor as yourself." (Lev. 19:18, NIV)

2. The Lord hates cheating and delights in honesty. (Prov. 11:1, TLB)

3. The Lord detests differing weights, and dishonest scales do not please him. (Prov. 20:23, NIV)

4. "For God will judge you in the same way you judge others, and he will apply to you the same rules you apply to others." (Matt. 7:2, TEV)

5. "Stop judging by mere appearances, and make a right judgment." (John 7:24, NIV)

6. "And as you wish that men would do to you, do so to them." (Luke 6:31, RSV)

He also said to them, "Pay attention to what you hear! The same rules you use to judge others will be used by God to judge you—but with even greater severity." (Mark 4:24, TEV)

If a person has wronged me, do I deserve to be angry? Why should I forgive him/her?

1. "For if you forgive men when they sin against you, your heavenly Father will also forgive you. But if you do not forgive men their sins, your Father will not forgive your sins." (Matt. 6:14, 15, NIV)

2. Then Peter came to him and asked, "Sir, how often should I forgive a brother who sins against me? Seven times?" "No!" Jesus replied, "seventy times seven!" (Matt. 18:21, 22, TLB)

3. "The king was very angry, and he sent the servant to jail to be punished until he should pay back the whole amount." And Jesus concluded, "That is how my Father in heaven will treat every one of you unless you forgive your brother from your heart." (Matt. 18:34, 35, TEV)

4. "Be merciful, just as your Father is merciful. Forgive, and you will be forgiven." (Luke 6:36, 37, NIV)

5. "Forgive us our sins, for we also forgive everyone who sins against us." (Luke 11:4, NIV)

6. "If your brother sins, rebuke him, and if he repents, forgive him. If he sins against you seven times in one day, and each time he comes to you saying, 'I repent,' you must forgive him." (Luke 17:3, 4, TEV)

7. Be kind and compassionate to one another, forgiving each other, just as in Christ God forgave you. (Eph. 4:32, NIV)

8. Be gentle and ready to forgive; never hold grudges. Remember, the Lord forgave you, so you must forgive others. (Col. 3:13, TLB)

Blessed is he whose transgression is forgiven, whose sin is covered. Blessed is the man unto whom the Lord imputeth not iniquity, and in whose spirit there is no guile. (Ps. 32:1, 2, KJV)

So many people in the world have problems or needs and I can't solve them all. So why should I bother myself with showing compassion to anyone?

1. He is good to everyone, and his compassion is intertwined with everything he does. (Ps. 145:9, TLB)

2. "Though the mountains be shaken and the hills be removed, yet my unfailing love for you will not be shaken nor my covenant of peace be removed," says the Lord, who has compassion on you. (Isa. 54:10, NIV)

3. As he saw the crowds, his heart was filled with pity for them, because they were worried and helpless, like sheep without a shepherd. (Matt. 9:36, TEV)

4. When Jesus landed and saw a large crowd, he had compassion on them and healed their sick. (Matt. 14:14, NIV)

5. "And the lord of that slave felt compassion and released him and forgave him the debt." (Matt. 18:27, NASB)

6. "Then the righteous will answer him, 'Lord, when did we see you hungry and feed you, or thirsty and give you something to drink? When did we see you a stranger and invite you in, or needing clothes and clothe you? When did we see you sick or in prison and go to visit you?' The King will reply, 'I tell you the truth, whatever you did for one of the least of these brothers of mine, you did for me.' " (Matt. 25:37-40, NIV)

7. And when the Lord saw her, he had compassion on her and said to her, "Do not weep." (Luke 7:13, RSV)

8. "But a Samaritan, as he journeyed, came to where he was; and when he saw him, he had compassion, and went to him and bound up his wounds, pouring on oil and wine; then he set him on his own beast and brought him to an inn, and took care of him. Which of these three, do you think, proved neighbor to the man who fell among the robbers?" He said, "The one who showed mercy on him." And Jesus said to him, "Go and do likewise." (Luke 10:33, 34, 36, 37, RSV)

9. "So he got up and went to his father. But while he was still a long way off, his father saw him and was filled with compassion for him; he ran to his son, threw his arms around him and kissed him." (Luke 15:20, NIV)

10. Live in harmony with one another; do not be haughty, but associate with the lowly; never be conceited. (Rom. 12:16, RSV)

11. You are the people of God; he loved you and chose you for his own. So then you must clothe yourselves with compassion, kindness, humility, gentleness, and patience. (Col. 3:12, TEV)

12. The Lord is full of compassion and mercy. (James 5:11, NIV)

13. Finally, all of you, live in harmony with one another; be sympathetic, love as brothers, be compassionate and humble. (1 Pet. 3:8, NIV)

14. If a rich person sees his brother in need, yet closes his heart against his brother, how can he claim that he loves God? My children, our love should not be just words and talk; it must be true love, which shows itself in action. (1 John 3:17, 18, TEV)

I feel so guilty about what I did. Can God really forgive me?

1. "But you are a forgiving God, gracious and compassionate, slow to anger and abounding in love. Therefore you did not desert them." (Neh. 9:17, NIV)

2. What happiness for those whose guilt has been forgiven! What joys when sins are covered over! (Ps. 32:1, TLB)

3. He has removed our sins as far away from us as the east is from the west. (Ps. 103:12, TLB)

4. "I tell you, then, the great love she has shown proves

that her many sins have been forgiven. But whoever has been forgiven little shows only a little love. Then Jesus said to the woman, "Your sins are forgiven." (Luke 7:47, 48, TEV)

5. Jesus said, "Father, forgive them, for they do not know what they are doing." (Luke 23:34, NIV)

6. He rescued us from the power of darkness and brought us safe into the kingdom of his dear Son, by whom we are set free, that is, our sins are forgiven. (Col. 1:13, 14, TEV)

7. Then he gave you a share in the very life of Christ, for he forgave all your sins, and blotted out the charges proved against you, the list of his commandments which you had not obeyed. He took this list of sins and destroyed it by nailing it to Christ's cross. (Col. 2:13, 14, TLB)

8. But if we confess our sins to God, he will keep his promise and what is right—he will forgive us our sins and purify us from all our wrongdoing. (1 John 1:9, TEV)

9. I write to you, dear children, because your sins have been forgiven on account of his name. (1 John 2:12, NIV)

I can't find any church near me that seems good enough. Should I bother getting involved with one?

1. Yes, the body has many parts, not just one part. . . . All

of you together are the one body of Christ and each one of you is a separate and necessary part of it. (1 Cor. 12:14, 27, TLB)

2. Christ loved the church and gave his life for it. He did this to dedicate the church to God by his word, after making it clean by washing it in water, in order to present the church to himself, in all its beauty—pure and faultless, without spot or wrinkle or any other imperfection. (Eph. 5:25-27, TEV)

3. Let us not give up meeting together, as some are in the habit of doing, but let us encourage one another—and all the more as you see the Day approaching. (Heb. 10:25, NIV)

I was glad when they said unto me, Let us go into the house of the Lord. (Ps. 122:1, KJV)

My life is dull. School is a bore. My job doesn't challenge me. There's nothing to do at home, and Bible reading and church services seem dry. How can I be enthusiastic?

1. "And you shall love the Lord your God with all your heart, and with all your soul, and with all your might." (Deut. 6:5, RSV)

2. And David danced before the Lord with all his might. (2 Sam. 6:14, RSV)

3. Then David and all the people danced before the

Lord with great enthusiasm, accompanied by singing and by zithers, harps, tambourines, cymbals, and trumpets. (1 Chron. 13:8, TLB)

4. Whatever your hand finds to do, do it with all your might. (Eccles. 9:10, NIV)

5. "Love the Lord your God with all your heart and with all your soul and with all your mind and with all your strength." (Mark 12:30, NIV)

6. Never be lazy in your work but serve the Lord enthusiastically. (Rom. 12:11, TLB)

7. Whatever you do, work at it with all your heart, as working for the Lord, not for men. (Col. 3:23, NIV)

8. We do not want you to become lazy. (Heb. 6:12, NIV)

When I am mistreated or misunderstood I want to get even. What should I do?

1. "Happy are you when people hate you, reject you, insult you, and say that you are evil, all because of the Son of Man! Be glad when that happens and dance for joy, because a great reward is kept for you in heaven." (Luke 6:22, 23, TEV)

2. "But I tell you who hear me: Love your enemies, do good to those who hate you, bless those who curse you, pray for those who mistreat you." (Luke 6:27, 28, NIV)

3. Don't quarrel with anyone. Be at peace with everyone, just as much as possible. (Rom. 12:18, TLB)

4. Do not take revenge, my friends, but leave room for God's wrath, for it is written: "It is mine to avenge; I will repay," says the Lord. On the contrary: If your enemy is hungry, feed him; if he is thirsty, give him something to drink. In doing this, you will heap burning coals on his head. (Rom. 12:19, 20, NIV)

5. Bear with each other and forgive whatever grievances you may have against one another. Forgive as the Lord forgave you. (Col. 3:13, NIV)

6. Again I say, don't get involved in foolish arguments which only upset people and make them angry. God's people must not be quarrelsome; they must be gentle, patient teachers of those who are wrong. Be humble when you are trying to teach those who are mixed up concerning the truth. For if you talk meekly and courteously to them they are more likely, with God's help, to turn away from their wrong ideas and believe what is true. (2 Tim. 2:23-25, TLB)

7. Finally, all of you, live in harmony with one another; be sympathetic, love as brothers, be compassionate and humble. Do not repay evil with evil or insult with insult, but with blessing, because to this you were called so that you may inherit a blessing. (1 Pet. 3:8, 9, NIV)

8. Happy are you if you are insulted because you are Christ's followers; this means that the glorious Spirit, the Spirit of God, is resting on you. If any of you suffers, it must not be because he is a murderer or a thief or a

criminal or meddles in other people's affairs. However, if you suffer because you are a Christian, don't be ashamed of it, but thank God that you bear Christ's name. (1 Pet. 4:14-16, TEV)

A soft answer turneth away wrath: but grievous words stir up anger. (Prov. 15:1, KJV)

VIII. Living with Others

Whenever I see a handicapped person I feel sorry for him/her and would like to talk to or help him/her. But I'm afraid of what my friends would think.

1. "You must not curse the deaf nor trip up a blind man as he walks. Fear your God; I am Jehovah!" (Lev. 19:14, TLB)

2. "Cursed is he who takes advantage of a blind man." (Deut. 27:18, TLB)

3. "I served as eyes for the blind and feet for the lame." (Job 29:15, TLB)

4. You made all the delicate, inner parts of my body, and knit them together in my mother's womb. Thank you for making me so wonderfully complex! It is amazing to think about. Your workmanship is marvelous—and how well I know it. You were there while I was being formed in utter seclusion! You saw me before I was born and scheduled each day of my life before I began to breathe. (Ps. 139:13-16, TLB)

5. His disciples asked him, "Teacher, whose sin caused him to be born blind? Was it his own or his parents' sin?"

Jesus answered, "His blindness has nothing to do with his sins or his parents' sins. He is blind so that God's power might be seen at work in him." (John 9:2, 3, TEV)

6. And whatever you do or say, let it be as a representative of the Lord Jesus, and come with him into the presence of God the Father to give him your thanks. (Col. 3:17, TLB)

It seems that my grandparents and other old people only want to criticize teenagers or talk about the "good old days." Why should I be kind to them?

1. "Rise in the presence of the aged, show respect for the elderly." (Lev. 19:32, NIV)

2. Never speak sharply to an older man, but plead with him respectfully just as though he were your own father. Talk to the younger men as you would to much loved brothers. Treat the older women as mothers. (1 Tim. 5:1, 2, TLB)

3. But if a widow has children or grandchildren, these should learn first of all to put their religion into practice by caring for their own family and so repaying their parents and grandparents, for this is pleasing to God. (1 Tim. 5:4, NIV)

4. If anyone does not provide for his relatives, and especially for his immediate family, he has denied the faith and is worse than an unbeliever. (1 Tim. 5:8, NIV)

People often ask to "borrow" my things, but I'm afraid they won't be returned. Isn't it wiser to keep my possessions so they aren't stolen or misused?

1. "If you have two coats," he replied, "give one to the poor. If you have extra food, give it away to those who are hungry." (Luke 3:11, TLB)

2. All the believers continued together in close fellowship and shared their belongings with one another. (Acts 2:44, TEV)

For God so loved the world, that he *gave.* . . . (John 3:16, KJV)

Is it really wrong to take home, occasionally, a few items from the office? Or to pocket something at the store? After all, those big corporations make their millions, so what difference can a few cents make?

1. "You shall not steal." (Ex. 20:15)

2. Ye shall not steal, neither deal falsely, neither lie one to another. (Lev. 19:11, KJV)

3. If you see your brother's ox or sheep straying, do not ignore it but be sure to take it back to him. If the brother does not live near you or if you do not know who he is, take it home with you and keep it until he comes looking

for it. Then give it back to him. Do the same if you find your brother's donkey or his cloak or anything he loses. Do not ignore it. (Deut. 22:1-3, NIV)

4. Do for others just what you want them to do for you. (Luke 6:31, TEV)

5. Let him that stole steal no more: but rather let him labour, working with his hands the thing which is good, that he may have to give to him that needeth. (Eph. 4:28, KJV)

Both in our neighborhood and church we have so many mothers without husbands and kids without fathers at home. Do I have any responsibility toward them?

1. "Do not take advantage of a widow or an orphan." (Ex. 22:22, NIV)

2. He defends the cause of the fatherless and the widow. (Deut. 10:18, NIV)

3. "Cursed is the man who withholds justice from the alien, the fatherless or the widow." (Deut. 27:19, NIV)

4. A father to the fatherless, a defender of widows, is God in his holy dwelling. (Ps. 68:5, NIV)

5. The Lord watches over the alien and sustains the fatherless and the widow. (Ps. 146:9, NIV)

6. "Defend the cause of the fatherless, plead the case of the widow." (Isa. 1:17, NIV)

7. "Do not oppress the widow or the fatherless, the alien or the poor." (Zech. 7:10, NIV)

8. Give proper recognition to those widows who are really in need. (1 Tim. 5:3, NIV)

9. But if a widow has children or grandchildren, these should learn first of all to put their religion into practice by caring for their own family and so repaying their parents and grandparents, for this is pleasing to God. (1 Tim. 5:4, NIV)

10. What God the Father considers to be pure and genuine religion is this: to take care of orphans and widows in their suffering, and to keep oneself from being corrupted by the world. (James 1:27, TEV)

The eternal God is thy refuge, and underneath are the everlasting arms. (Deut. 33:27, KJV)

I've seen what happens to people when they get overly enthusiastic about a cause. People will reject me for being too strong a Christian, a fanatic, so wouldn't it be better to "play it cool" so I can maintain communication with them?

1. "Blessed are those who are persecuted because of

righteousness, for theirs is the kingdom of heaven. Rejoice and be glad, because great is your reward in heaven, for in the same way they persecuted the prophets who were before you." (Matt. 5:10, 12, NIV)

2. "So a pupil should be satisified to become like his teacher, and a slave like his master. If the head of the family is called Beelzebul, the members of the family will be called by even worse names!" (Matt. 10:25, TEV)

3. "Happy are you when people hate you, reject you, insult you, and say that you are evil, all because of the Son of Man!" (Luke 6:22, TEV)

4. "If the world hates you, keep in mind that it hated me first. If you belonged to the world, it would love you as its own. As it is, you do not belong to the world, but I have chosen you out of the world. This is why the world hates you. Remember the words I spoke to you: 'No servant is greater than his master.' If they persecuted me, they will persecute you also. If they obeyed my teaching, they will obey yours also." (John 15:18-20, NIV)

Rather be glad that you are sharing Christ's sufferings, so that you may be full of joy when his glory is revealed. Happy are you if you are insulted because you are Christ's followers; this means that the glorious Spirit, the Spirit of God, is resting on you. (1 Pet. 4:13, 14, TEV)

Sometimes it just seems better to save my reputation than to be honest and own up to

my mistakes. Is it all right to cheat once in a while?

1. "In all your transactions you must use accurate scales and honest measurements, so that you will have a long, good life in the land the Lord your God is giving you." (Deut. 25:13-15, TLB)

2. "I know, my God, that you test the heart and are pleased with integrity. All these things have I given willingly and with honest intent." (1 Chron. 29:17, NIV)

3. Thou destroyest those who speak lies; the Lord abhors bloodthirsty and deceitful men. (Ps. 5:6, RSV)

4. Who may climb the mountain of the Lord and enter where he lives? Who may stand before the Lord? Only those with pure hands and hearts, who do not practice dishonesty and lying. (Ps. 24:3, 4, TLB)

5. No one who practices deceit will dwell in my house; no one who speaks falsely will stand in my presence. (Ps. 101:7, NIV)

6. The Lord detests lying lips, but he delights in men who are truthful. (Prov. 12:22, NIV)

7. Bread gained by deceit is sweet to a man, but afterward his mouth will be full of gravel. (Prov. 20:17, RSV)

8. The Lord loathes all cheating and dishonesty. (Prov. 20:23, TLB)

9. He had done no violence, and there was no deceit in his mouth. (Isa. 53:9, RSV)

10. "Do to others as you would have them do to you." (Luke 6:31, NIV)

11. Rather, we have renounced secret and shameful ways; we do not use deception, nor do we distort the word of God. On the contrary, by setting forth the truth plainly we commend ourselves to every man's conscience in the sight of God. (2 Cor. 4:2, NIV)

And whatsoever ye do in word or deed, do all in the name of the Lord Jesus, giving thanks to God and the Father by him. (Col. 3:17, KJV)

I'm sometimes late to work and I like to take it easy on the job. But I work as hard as the others. Isn't that good enough?

1. The faithfulness of the Lord endures forever. (Ps. 117:2, NIV)

2. "Whoever is faithful in small matters will be faithful in large ones; whoever is dishonest in small matters will be dishonest in large ones." (Luke 16:10, TEV)

3. Now it is required that those who have been given a trust must prove faithful. (1 Cor. 4:2, NIV)

4. Servants, obey in all things your masters according to the flesh; not with eyeservice, as menpleasers; but in singleness of heart, fearing God: and whatsoever ye do, do it heartily, as to the Lord, and not unto men; knowing

that of the Lord ye shall receive the reward of the inheritance: for ye serve the Lord Christ. (Col. 3:22-24, KJV)

5. The one who calls you is faithful and he will do it. (1 Thess. 5:24, NIV)

I'm ashamed of my parents. And I don't think they even love me. Why should I show them any respect?

1. "Cursed is anyone who despises his father or mother." And all the people shall reply, "Amen." (Deut. 27:16, TLB)

2. They were filled with all manner of wickedness ... slanderers, haters of God, insolent, haughty, boastful, inventors of evil, disobedient to parents. Though they know God's decree that those who do such things deserve to die, they not only do them but approve those who practice them. (Rom. 1:29, 30, 32, RSV)

3. But if any widow have children or nephews, let them learn first to show piety at home, and to requite their parents: for that is good and acceptable before God. (1 Tim. 5:4, KJV)

4. But mark this: There will be terrible times in the last days. People will be lovers of themselves, lovers of money, boastful, proud, abusive, disobedient to their parents, ungrateful, unholy. (2 Tim. 3:1, 2, NIV)

My son, do not forget my teaching, but let your heart keep my commandments. . . . So you will find favor and good repute in the sight of God and man. (Prov. 3:1, 4, NASB)

When my brother/sister starts treating me properly, I'll do the same. That seems fair, doesn't it?

1. How wonderful it is, how pleasant, when brothers live in harmony! (Ps. 133:1, TLB)

2. "But I say to you that every one who is angry with his brother shall be liable to judgment." (Matt. 5:22, RSV)

3. Then Peter came to him and asked, "Sir, how often should I forgive a brother who sins against me? Seven times?" "No!" Jesus replied, "seventy times seven!" (Matt. 18:21, 22, TLB)

4. "If your brother sins, rebuke him, and if he repents, forgive him. If he sins against you seven times in one day, and each time he comes to you saying, 'I repent,' you must forgive him." (Luke 17:3, 4, TEV)

5. If it is possible, as far as it depends on you, live at peace with everyone. (Rom. 12:18, NIV)

6. Love is not rude, it is not self-seeking, it is not easily

angered, it keeps no record of wrongs. . . . It always protects, always trusts, always hopes, always perseveres.
(1 Cor. 13:5, 7, NIV)

7. Get rid of all bitterness, passion, and anger. No more
shouting or insults, no more hateful feelings of any sort.
Instead, be kind and tender-hearted to one another, and
forgive one another, as God has forgiven you through
Christ. (Eph. 4:31, 32, TEV)

8. If anyone says "I love God," but keeps on hating his
brother, he is a liar; for if he doesn't love his brother who
is right there in front of him, how can he love God whom
he has never seen? (1 John 4:20, TLB)

For thou, Lord, art good, and ready to forgive. (Ps.
86:5, KJV)

I can't seem to control my temper. Should I force myself to hold such feelings inside?

1. Refrain from anger and turn from wrath. (Ps. 37:8,
NIV)

2. A quick-tempered man does foolish things. (Prov.
14:17, NIV)

3. A patient man has great understanding, but a quick-
tempered man displays folly. (Prov. 14:29, NIV)

4. Do not make friends with a hot-tempered man, do not

associate with one easily angered, or you may learn his ways and get yourself ensnared. (Prov. 22:24, 25, NIV)

5. Now the works of the flesh are plain: fornication, impurity ... anger, selfishness.... I warn you, as I warned you before, that those who do such things shall not inherit the kingdom of God. (Gal. 5:19-21, RSV)

6. Get rid of all bitterness, rage and anger, brawling and slander, along with every form of malice. (Eph. 4:31, NIV)

7. I desire then that in every place the men should pray, lifting holy hands without anger or quarreling. (1 Tim. 2:8, RSV)

8. For God did not give us a spirit of timidity but a spirit of power and love and self-control. (1 Tim. 1:7, RSV)

9. My dear brothers, take note of this: Everyone should be quick to listen, slow to speak and slow to become angry, for man's anger does not bring about the righteous life that God desires. (James 1:19, 20, NIV)

I can do all things through Christ which strengtheneth me. (Phil. 4:13, KJV)

I realize God, in some way, provided the money that I have. But why should I give any to Him? If He owns all things, why should He want something from me?

1. "There are many among you who are poor, you must not shut your heart or hand against them; you must lend to them as much as they need." (Deut. 15:7, 8, TLB)

2. When you help the poor you are lending to the Lord—and he pays wonderful interest on your loan. (Prov. 19:17, TLB)

3. He who gives to the poor will lack nothing, but he who closes his eyes to them receives many curses. (Prov. 28:27, NIV)

4. "Bring the whole tithe into the storehouse, that there may be food in my house. Test me in this," says the Lord Almighty, "and see if I will not throw open the floodgates of heaven and pour out so much blessing that you will not have room enough for it." (Mal. 3:10, NIV)

5. "Give to others, and God will give to you. Indeed you will receive a full measure, a generous helping, poured into your hands—all that you can hold. The measure you use for others is the one that God will use for you. (Luke 6:38, TEV)

6. "In everything I did, I showed you that by this kind of hard work we must help the weak, remembering the words the Lord Jesus himself said: 'It is more blessed to give than to receive.' " (Acts 20:35, NIV)

7. If God has given you money, be generous in helping others with it. . . . (Rom. 12:8, TLB)

8. On every Lord's Day each of you should put aside something from what you have earned during the week,

and use it for this offering. The amount depends on how much the Lord has helped you earn. (1 Cor. 16:2, TLB)

9. Each one should give, then, as he has decided, not with regret or out of a sense of duty; for God loves the one who gives gladly. (2 Cor. 9:7, TEV)

But this I say, He which soweth sparingly shall reap also sparingly; and he which soweth bountifully shall reap also bountifully. (2 Cor. 9:6, KJV)

It's easy to pick up a lot of coarse expressions and jokes. If I use them among people who don't mind, is that acceptable?

1. Lord, who may go and find refuge and shelter in your tabernacle up on your holy hill? Anyone who leads a blameless life and is truly sincere. Anyone who refuses to slander others, does not listen to gossip, never harms his neighbor, speaks out against sin, criticizes those committing it, commends the faithful followers of the Lord, keeps a promise even if it ruins him. (Ps. 15:1-4, TLB)

2. Whoever of you loves life and desires to see many good days, keep your tongue from evil and your lips from speaking lies. (Ps. 34:12, 13, NIV)

3. The words of the wicked lie in wait for blood, but the speech of the upright rescues them. (Prov. 12:6, NIV)

4. From the fruit of his lips a man is filled with good things as surely as the work of his hands rewards him. (Prov. 12:14, NIV)

5. A gentle answer turns away wrath, but a harsh word stirs up anger. (Prov. 15:1, NIV)

6. Gold there is, and rubies in abundance, but lips that speak knowledge are a rare jewel. (Prov. 20:15, NIV)

7. He who guards his mouth and his tongue keeps himself from calamity. (Prov. 21:23, NIV)

8. "If anyone publicly acknowledges me as his friend, I will openly acknowledge him as my friend before my Father in heaven." (Matt. 10:32, TLB)

9. "For by your words you will be justified, and by your words you will be condemned." (Matt. 12:37, RSV)

Sometimes I weary of inviting guests to our home and entertaining them. How much hospitality is expected of me? Must I always be friendly to strangers?

1. Share with God's people who are in need. Practice hospitality. (Rom. 12:13, NIV)

2. Now the overseer must be above reproach, the husband of but one wife, temperate, self-controlled, respectable, hospitable, able to teach. (1 Tim. 3:2, NIV)

3. Rather he must be hospitable, one who loves what is good, who is self-controlled, upright, holy and disciplined. (Titus 1:8, NIV)

4. Do not forget to entertain strangers, for by so doing some people have entertained angels without knowing it. (Heb. 13:2, NIV)

5. Offer hospitality to one another without grumbling. (1 Pet. 4:9, NIV)

And the Lord appeared unto [Abraham] in the plains of Mamre: and he sat in the tent door in the heat of the day; and he lift up his eyes and looked, and, lo, three men stood by him: and when he saw them, he ran to meet them from the tent door and bowed himself toward the ground, and said . . . Let a little water, I pray you, be fetched, and wash your feet, and rest yourselves under the tree: and I will fetch a morsel of bread, and comfort ye your hearts; after that ye shall pass on: for therefore are ye come to your servant. (Gen. 18:1-5, KJV)

IX. Living with Myself (inner expression)

I'm trying to decide what my life goals should be. What are the most important things I should consider?

1. I said to the Lord, "You are my Lord; apart from you, I have no good thing." (Ps. 16:2, NIV)

2. One thing I ask of the Lord, this is what I seek: that I may dwell in the house of the Lord all the days of my life, to gaze upon the beauty of the Lord and to seek him in his temple. (Ps. 27:4, NIV)

3. Delight yourself in the Lord, and he will give you the desires of your heart. (Ps. 37:4, NIV)

4. Whom have I in heaven but you? And being with you, I desire nothing on earth. (Ps. 73:25, NIV)

5. "But seek first his kingdom and his righteousness, and all these things will be given to you as well." (Matt. 6:33, NIV)

6. My deep desire and hope is that I shall never fail in my duty, but that at all times, and especially right now, I shall be full of courage, so that with my whole being I shall bring honor to Christ, whether I live or die. (Phil. 1:20, TEV)

7. For I live in eager expectation and hope ... that I will always be an honor to Christ, whether I live or whether I must die. For to me, living means opportunities for Christ, and dying—well, that's better yet! (Phil. 1:20, 21, TLB)

8. What is more, I consider everything a loss compared to the surpassing greatness of knowing Christ Jesus my Lord, for whose sake I have lost all things. I consider them rubbish, that I may gain Christ. ... I want to know Christ and the power of his resurrection and the fellowship of sharing in his sufferings, becoming like him in his death. (Phil. 3:8, 10, NIV)

9. The one thing I do, however, is to forget what is behind me and do my best to reach what is ahead. So I run straight toward the goal in order to win the prize, which is God's call through Christ Jesus to the life above. (Phil. 3:13, 14, TEV)

10. Let us fix our eyes on Jesus, the author and perfecter of our faith. (Heb. 12:2, NIV)

These days a person's got to look out for himself. Isn't loyalty an archaic concept?

1. I will sing of loyalty and of justice; to thee, O Lord, I will sing. (Ps. 101:1, RSV)

2. Let not loyalty and faithfulness forsake you; bind them about your neck, write them on the tablet of your heart. (Prov. 3:3, RSV)

3. By loyalty and faithfulness iniquity is atoned for; and by the fear of the Lord a man avoids evil. (Prov. 16:6, RSV)

4. Many a man proclaims his own loyalty, but a faithful man who can find? (Prov. 20:6, RSV)

5. The one thing required of such a servant is that he be faithful to his master. (1 Cor. 4:2, TEV)

I find that I'm not a very courageous person. How can I develop fortitude?

1. Then the Lord said to Joshua, "Do not be afraid; do not be discouraged." (Josh. 8:1, NIV)

2. For I cried to him and he answered me! He freed me from all my fears. (Ps. 34:4, TLB)

3. The wicked man flees though no one pursues, but the righteous are as bold as a lion. (Prov. 28:1, NIV)

4. Strengthen the feeble hands, steady the knees that give way; say to those with fearful hearts, "Be strong, do not fear." (Isa. 35:3, 4, NIV)

5. "Why are you so frightened?" Jesus answered. "What little faith you have!" (Matt. 8:26, TEV)

6. "Do not be afraid, little flock, for your Father has been pleased to give you the kingdom." (Luke 12:32, NIV)

7. For God hath not given us the spirit of fear; but of

power, and of love, and of a sound mind. (2 Tim. 1:7, KJV)

8. That is why we can say without any doubt or fear, "The Lord is my Helper and I am not afraid of anything that mere man can do to me." (Heb. 13:6, TLB)

9. We need have no fear of someone who loves us perfectly; his perfect love for us eliminates all dread of what he might do to us. If we are afraid, it is for fear of what he might do to us, and shows that we are not fully convinced that he really loves us. (1 John 4:18, TLB)

10. But the fearful, and unbelieving, and the abominable, and murderers, and whoremongers, and sorcerers, and idolaters, and all liars, shall have their part in the lake which burneth with fire and brimstone: which is the second death. (Rev. 21:8, KJV)

No weapon that is formed against thee shall prosper; and every tongue that shall rise against thee in judgment thou shalt condemn. This is the heritage of the servants of the Lord, and their righteousness is of me, saith the Lord. (Isa. 54:17, KJV)

How can I overcome feelings of loneliness?

1. To you, O Lord, I lift up my soul; in you I trust, O my God. (Ps. 25:1, 2, NIV)

2. For the Lord loves the just and will not forsake his

faithful ones. (Ps. 37:28, NIV)

3. He is always kind and loving to me; he is my fortress, my tower of strength and safety, my deliverer. He stands before me as a shield. He subdues my people under me. (Ps. 144:2, TLB)

4. For the mountains may depart and the hills disappear, but my kindness shall not leave you. My promise of peace for you will never be broken, says the Lord who has mercy upon you. (Isa. 54:10, TLB)

5. "The Lord your God is with you, he is mighty to save. He will take great delight in you, he will quiet you with his love, he will rejoice over you with singing." (Zeph. 3:17, NIV)

6. "And surely, I will be with you always, to the very end of the age." (Matt. 28:20, NIV)

7. "And I will ask the Father, and he will give you another Counselor to be with you forever. I will not leave you as orphans; I will come to you." (John 14:16, 18, NIV)

8. God has said, "Never will I leave you; never will I forsake you." (Heb. 13:5, NIV)

I feel as if I'm the greatest failure in the world. Is there any way to change this feeling?

1. I cannot understand how you can bother with mere

puny man, to pay any attention to him! And yet you have made him only a little lower than the angels. (Ps. 8:4, 5, TLB)

2. You are all sons of God through faith in Christ Jesus. (Gal. 3:26, NIV)

3. For we are God's workmanship, created in Christ Jesus to do good works. (Eph. 2:10, NIV)

4. So then you are no longer strangers and sojourners, but you are fellow citizens with the saints and members of the household of God. (Eph. 2:19, RSV)

5. But you are a chosen race, a royal priesthood, a holy nation, God's own people, that you may declare the wonderful deeds of him who called you out of darkness into his marvelous light. (1 Pet. 2:9, RSV)

6. Once you were less than nothing; now you are God's own. (1 Pet. 2:10, TLB)

I can't endure the pressure of this task any longer. Should I quit?

1. "I said, 'You are my servant'; I have chosen you and have not rejected you. So do not fear, for I am with you; do not be dismayed, for I am your God. I will strengthen you and help you; I will uphold you with my righteous right hand." (Isa. 41:9, 10, NIV)

2. And we also boast of our troubles, because we know

that trouble produces endurance, endurance brings God's approval, and his approval creates hope. (Rom. 5:3, 4, TEV)

3. And as for you, brothers, never tire of doing what is right. (2 Thess. 3:13, NIV)

4. Endure hardship with us like a good soldier of Christ Jesus. (2 Tim. 2:3, NIV)

5. For you have need of endurance, so that you may do the will of God and receive what is promised. (Heb. 10:36, RSV)

6. Therefore, since we are surrounded by such a great cloud of witnesses, let us throw off everything that hinders and the sin that so easily entangles, and let us run with perseverance the race marked out for us. Let us fix our eyes on Jesus, the author and perfecter of our faith, who for the joy set before him endured the cross, scorning its shame, and sat down at the right hand of the throne of God. Consider him who endured such opposition from sinful men, so that you will not grow weary and lose heart. (Heb. 12:1-3, NIV)

7. Consider it pure joy, my brothers, whenever you face trials of many kinds, because you know that the testing of your faith develops perseverance. (James 1:2, 3, NIV)

What's wrong with protecting my own rights? I don't think I'm being selfish.

1. Love one another with brotherly affection; outdo one

another in showing honor. (Rom. 12:10, RSV)

2. Nobody should seek his own good, but the good of others. (1 Cor. 10:24, NIV)

3. Now the works of the flesh are plain: fornication, impurity, licentiousness, idolatry, sorcery, enmity, strife, jealousy, anger, *selfishness*, dissension, party spirit, envy, drunkenness, carousing, and the like. (Gal. 5:19-21, RSV)

4. Bear one another's burdens, and so fulfil the law of Christ. (Gal. 6:2, RSV)

5. Don't be selfish or proud, but humbly treat others as better than yourselves. Each of you, be interested not only in your own things but also in those of others. Think just as Christ Jesus thought. (Phil. 2:3-5, Beck)

6. I have no one like [Timothy], who will be genuinely anxious for your welfare. They all look after their own interests, not those of Jesus Christ. (Phil. 2:20, 21, RSV)

7. You will be doing the right thing if you obey the law of the Kingdom, which is found in the scripture, "Love your neighbor as you love yourself." (James 2:8, TEV)

8. But if any one has the world's goods and sees his brother in need, yet closes his heart against him, how does God's love abide in him? Little children, let us not love in word or speech but in deed and in truth. (1 John 3:17, 18, RSV)

What's wrong with committing a "sin" if no-

body else knows about it?

1. But if you don't do as you have said, then you will have sinned against the Lord, and you may be sure that your sin will catch up with you. (Num. 32:23, TLB)

2. "But now, instead, you give me so few steps upon the stage of life, and notice every mistake I make." (Job 14:16, TLB)

3. Who can discern his errors? Forgive my hidden faults. (Ps. 19:12, NIV)

4. He knows the secrets of every heart. (Ps. 44:21, TLB)

5. For I know my transgressions, and my sin is always before me. (Ps. 51:3, NIV)

6. You know my folly, O God; my guilt is not hidden from you. (Ps. 69:5, NIV)

7. You have set our iniquities before you, our secret sins in the light of your presence. (Ps. 90:8, NIV)

8. I can never be lost to your Spirit! I can never get away from my God! If I go up to heaven, you are there; if I go down to the place of the dead, you are there. If I try to hide in the darkness, the night becomes light around me. For even darkness cannot hide from God; to you the night shines as bright as day. Darkness and night are both alike to you. (Ps. 139:7, 8, 11, 12, TLB)

9. For I am closely watching you and I see every sin. You cannot hope to hide from me. (Jer. 16:17, TLB)

10. "There is nothing concealed that will not be disclosed, or hidden that will not be made known." (Luke 12:2, NIV)

11. This will take place on the day when God will judge men's secrets through Jesus Christ, as my gospel declares. (Rom. 2:16, NIV)

12. The sins of some men are conspicuous, pointing to judgment, but the sins of others appear later. (1 Tim. 5:24, RSV)

I don't feel self-assured when I'm with people. Is there a solution to my problem?

1. "If I have put my trust in gold or said to pure gold, 'You are my security,' then these also would be sins to be judged, for I would have been unfaithful to God on high." (Job 31:24, 28, NIV)

2. The Lord is my light and my salvation—whom shall I fear? The Lord is the stronghold of my life—of whom shall I be afraid? Though an army besiege me, my heart will not fear; though war break out against me, even then will I be confident. (Ps. 27:1, 3, NIV)

3. It is better to trust in the Lord than to put confidence in man. (Ps. 118:8, KJV)

4. You need not be afraid of disaster or the plots of wicked men, for the Lord is with you; he protects you. (Prov. 3:25, 26, TLB)

5. In the fear of the Lord is strong confidence: and his children shall have a place of refuge. (Prov. 14:26, KJV)

6. For thus saith the Lord God, the Holy One of Israel; In returning and rest shall ye be saved; in quietness and in confidence shall be your strength. (Isa. 30:15, KJV)

7. Therefore we are always confident. (2 Cor. 5:6, NIV)

8. In him and through faith in him we may approach God with freedom and confidence. (Eph. 3:12, NIV)

9. For I am confident of this very thing, that He who began a good work in you will perfect it until the day of Christ Jesus. (Phil. 1:6, NASB)

10. For it is we who are the circumcision, we who worship by the Spirit of God, who glory in Christ Jesus, and who put no confidence in the flesh. (Phil. 3:3, NIV)

11. Dear friends, if our hearts do not condemn us, we have confidence before God. (1 John 3:21, NIV)

12. And this is the confidence that we have in him, that, if we ask any thing according to his will, he heareth us. (1 John 5:14, KJV)

Other people seem to have so much more than I. Why should I be thankful?

1. "Is God's comfort too little for you? Is his gentleness too rough? What is this you are doing, getting carried

away by your anger, with flashing eyes? And you turn against God and say all these evil things against him." (Job 15:11-13, TLB)

2. Do not fret because of evil men or be envious of those who do wrong. (Ps. 37:1, NIV)

3. Better the little that the righteous have than the wealth of many wicked. (Ps. 37:16, NIV)

4. But who are you, my friend, to talk back to God? A clay pot does not ask the man who made it, "Why did you make me like this?" (Rom. 9:20, TEV)

5. We must not complain, as some of them did—and they were destroyed by the Angel of Death. (1 Cor. 10:10, TEV)

6. Do everything without complaining or arguing. (Phil. 2:14, NIV)

7. And I am not saying this because I feel neglected; for I have learned to be satisfied with what I have. I know what it is to be in need, and what it is to have more than enough. I have learned this secret, so that anywhere, at any time, I am content, whether I am full or hungry, whether I have too much or too little. I have the strength to face all conditions by the power that Christ gives me. (Phil. 4:11-13, TEV)

I'm in too big a hurry to wait around for God to do something; I can't afford to be patient.

Is it all right if I hurry up the process?

1. Rest in the Lord; wait patiently for him to act. (Ps. 37:7, TLB)

2. I waited patiently for God to help me; then he listened and heard my cry. (Ps. 40:1, TLB)

3. Do you see a man who speaks in haste? There is more hope for a fool than for him. (Prov. 29:20, NIV)

4. The patient in spirit is better than the proud in spirit. (Eccles. 7:8, RSV)

5. He will give each one whatever his deeds deserve. He will give eternal life to those who patiently do the will of God. (Rom. 2:6, 7, TLB)

6. Be glad for all God is planning for you. Be patient in trouble, and prayerful always. (Rom. 12:12, TLB)

7. But the fruit of the Spirit is love, joy, peace, patience, kindness, goodness, faithfulness. (Gal. 5:22, NIV)

8. Be patient with everyone. (1 Thess. 5:14, NIV)

9. May the Lord bring you into an ever deeper understanding of the love of God and of the patience that comes from Christ. (2 Thess. 3:5, TLB)

10. Oh, Timothy, you are God's man. Run from all these evil things and work instead at what is right and good, learning to trust him and love others, and to be patient and gentle. (1 Tim. 6:11, TLB)

11. God's people must not be quarrelsome; they must be gentle, patient teachers of those who are wrong. (2 Tim. 2:24, TLB)

12. And so after waiting patiently, Abraham received what was promised. (Heb. 6:13, 15, NIV)

13. Be patient, then, brothers, until the Lord's coming. See how the farmer waits for the land to yield its valuable crop and how patient he is for the autumn and spring rains. (James 5:7, 8, NIV)

14. But do not forget this one thing, dear friends: With the Lord a day is like a thousand years, and a thousand years are like a day. The Lord is not slow in keeping his promise, as some understand slowness. He is patient with you, not wanting anyone to perish, but everyone to come to repentance. (2 Pet. 3:8, 9, NIV)

X. Discontentment

School seems such a waste of time; I could be out earning money or having fun. Why should I keep studying so hard?

1. How does a man become wise? The first step is to trust and reverence the Lord! Only fools refuse to be taught.... What you learn from them will stand you in good stead; it will gain you many honors. (Prov. 1:7, 9, TLB)

2. How long will you simple ones love your simple ways? How long will mockers delight in mockery and fools hate knowledge? (Prov. 1:22, NIV)

3. Wise men lay up knowledge. (Prov. 10:14, RSV)

4. Hear counsel, and receive instruction, that thou mayest be wise in thy latter end. (Prov. 19:20, KJV)

5. Then the king ordered Ashpenaz, chief of his court officials, to bring in some of the Israelites from the royal family and the nobility—young men without any physical defect, handsome, showing aptitude for every kind of learning, well informed, quick to understand, and qualified to serve in the king's palace. He was to teach them the language and literature of the Babylonians. (Dan. 1:3, 4, NIV)

6. Jesus replied: "Love the Lord your God with all your heart and with all your soul and with all your mind." (Matt. 22:37, NIV)

7. Moses was educated in all the wisdom of the Egyptians and was powerful in speech and action. (Acts 7:22, NIV)

8. And as he thus made his defense, Festus said with a loud voice, "Paul, you are mad; your great learning is turning you mad." (Acts 26:24, RSV)

9. Try to learn what is pleasing to the Lord. (Eph. 5:10, RSV)

10. Study to show thyself approved unto God, a workman that needeth not to be ashamed, rightly dividing the word of truth. (2 Tim. 2:15, KJV)

When wisdom entereth into thine heart, and knowledge is pleasant unto thy soul; discretion shall preserve thee, understanding shall keep thee. (Prov. 2:10, 11, KJV)

It doesn't seem fair that others, both good and evil, have so much more than I. Why doesn't God provide for me as He does for them?

1. "You must not be envious of your neighbor's house,

or want to sleep with his wife, or want to own his slaves, oxen, donkeys, or anything else he has." (Ex. 20:17, TLB)

2. Do not fret because of evil men or be envious of those who do wrong; for like the grass they will soon wither, like green plants they will soon die away. Trust in the Lord and do good. (Ps. 37:1-3, NIV)

3. It is better to have little and be godly than to own an evil man's wealth. (Ps. 37:16, TLB)

4. The Lord takes care of those he has forgiven. Day by day the Lord observes the good deeds done by godly men, and gives them eternal rewards. He cares for them when times are hard; even in famine, they will have enough. (Ps. 37:17-19, TLB)

5. "Do not store up riches here on earth, where moths and rust destroy, and robbers break in and steal. Instead store up riches for yourselves in heaven, where moths and rust cannot destroy, and robbers cannot break in and steal." (Matt. 6:19, 20, TEV)

6. "He gave to each one according to his ability." (Matt. 25:15, TEV)

7. "But Abraham said to him, 'Son, remember that during your lifetime you had everything you wanted, and Lazarus had nothing. So now he is here being comforted and you are in anguish.'" (Luke 16:25, TLB)

8. I have learned how to get along happily whether I have much or little. I know how to live on almost nothing or

with everything. I have learned the secret of contentment in every situation, whether it be a full stomach or hunger, plenty or want; for I can do everything God asks me to with the help of Christ who gives me the strength and power. (Phil. 4:11-13, NIV)

Blessed is the man that walketh not in the counsel of the ungodly ... his delight is in the law of the Lord ... and whatsoever he doeth shall prosper. (Ps. 1:1-3, KJV)

I read and hear about people who seemingly get answers to all their prayers. I don't seem to get any answers. What's wrong?

1. So, when they cry out, he does not answer, because they are self-willed and proud. All to no purpose! God does not listen, the Almighty does not see. (Job 35:12, 13, NEB)

2. If I had cherished sin in my heart, the Lord would not have listened; (Ps. 66:18, NIV)

3. God doesn't listen to the prayers of men who flout the law. (Prov. 28:9, TLB)

4. "You will seek me and find me when you seek me with all your heart." (Jer. 29:13, NIV)

5. The Lord said to me, Man, these people have set their

hearts on their idols and keep their eyes fixed on the sinful things that cause their downfall. Am I to let such men
consult me? (Ezek. 14:2, 3, NEB)

6. "Don't recite the same prayer over and over as the
heathen do, who think prayers are answered only by re-
peating them again and again. Remember, your Father
knows exactly what you need even before you ask him!"
(Matt. 6:7, 8, TLB)

7. "We know that God does not listen to sinners. He lis-
tens to the godly man who does his will." (John 9:31,
NIV)

8. "If you remain in me and my words remain in you, ask
whatever you wish, and it will be given you." (John 15:7,
NIV)

9. But when you pray, you must believe and not doubt at
all. Whoever doubts is like a wave in the sea that is driven
and blown about by the wind. A person like that, unable
to make up his mind and undecided in all he does must
not think that he will receive anything from the Lord.
(James 1:6-8, TEV)

10. You do not have, because you do not ask God.
When you ask, you do not receive, because you ask with
wrong motives, that you may spend what you get on your
pleasures. (James 4:2, 3, NIV)

11. You husbands, also in living with your wives you
must recognize that they are the weaker sex and so you
must treat them with respect; for they also will receive, together with you, God's gift of life. Do this so that nothing
will interfere with your prayers. (1 Pet. 3:7, TEV)

12. This is the assurance we have in approaching God: that if we ask anything according to his will, he hears us. (1 John 5:14, NIV)

I feel as if everyone I know has tried or is using drugs, alcohol or tobacco, and none seems to be getting harmed by the stuff. Is it really so bad to use those things?

1. Wine gives false courage; hard liquor leads to brawls; what fools men are to let it master them, making them reel drunkenly down the street! (Prov. 20:1, TLB)

2. O my son, be wise and stay in God's paths; don't carouse with drunkards and gluttons, for they are on their way to poverty. (Prov. 23:19, 20, TLB)

3. Woe to those who are "heroes" when it comes to drinking, and boast about the liquor they can hold. (Isa. 5:22, TLB)

4. For sin shall not have dominion over you: for ye are not under the law, but under grace. (Rom. 6:14, KJV)

5. I can do anything I want to if Christ has not said no, but some of these things aren't good for me. Even if I am allowed to do them, I'll refuse to if I think they might get such a grip on me that I can't easily stop when I want to. (1 Cor. 6:12, TLB)

6. Haven't you yet learned that your body is the home of the Holy Spirit God gave you, and that he lives within

you? Your own body does not belong to you. For God has bought you with a great price. So use every part of your body to give glory back to God, because he owns it. (1 Cor. 6:19, 20, TLB)

7. So whether you eat or drink or whatever you do, do it all for the glory of God. (1 Cor. 10:31, NIV)

8. What human nature does is quite plain. It shows itself in immoral, filthy, and indecent actions. They are envious, get drunk, have orgies, and do other things like these. I warn you now as I have before: those who do these things will not possess the Kingdom of God. (Gal. 5:19, 21, TEV)

9. Do not get drunk with wine, which will only ruin you; instead, be filled with the Spirit. (Eph. 5:18, TEV)

10. No one hates his own body but lovingly cares for it, just as Christ cares for his body the church. (Eph. 5:29, TLB)

11. Dear brothers, you are only visitors here. Since your real home is in heaven I beg you to keep away from the evil pleasures of this world; they are not for you, for they fight against your very souls. (1 Pet. 2:11, TLB)

The only reward I get for obeying my parents is a dull evening at home. How can obedience possibly pay off?

1. "Honor your father and your mother, so that you may

live long in the land the Lord your God is giving you." (Ex. 20:12, NIV)

2. Honor your father and mother. This is the first of God's Ten Commandments that ends with a promise. And this is the promise: that if you honor your father and mother, yours will be a long life, full of blessing. (Eph. 6:2, 3, TLB)

3. Children, obey your parents in everything, for this pleases the Lord. (Col. 3:20, NIV)

The thought of dying scares me. What happens to people when they die?

1. He will swallow up death forever. The Sovereign Lord will wipe away the tears from all faces; he will remove the disgrace of his people from all the earth. The Lord has spoken. In that day they will say, "Surely this is our God; we trusted in him, and he saved us. This is the Lord, we trusted in him; let us rejoice and be glad in his salvation. (Isa. 25:8, 9, NIV)

2. For I am convinced that nothing can ever separate us from his love. Death can't, and life can't. The angels won't, and all the powers of hell itself cannot keep God's love away. Nothing will ever be able to separate us from the love of God demonstrated by our Lord Jesus Christ when he died for us. (Rom. 8:38, 39, TLB)

3. So when this takes place, and the mortal has been changed into the immortal, then the scripture will come

true: "Death is destroyed; victory is complete! Where, Death, is your victory? Where, Death, is your power to hurt?" But thanks be to God who gives us the victory through our Lord Jesus Christ! (1 Cor. 15:54, 55, 57, TEV)

4. For to me, living means opportunities for Christ, and dying—well, that's better yet! But if living will give me more opportunities to win people to Christ, then I really don't know which is better, to live or die! Sometimes I want to live and at other times I don't, for I long to go and be with Christ. How much happier for me than being here! (Phil. 1:21-23, TLB)

5. For the Lord himself will come down from heaven, with a loud command, with the voice of the archangel and with the trumpet call of God, and the dead in Christ will rise first. After that, we who are still alive and are left will be caught up with them in the clouds to meet the Lord in the air. And so we will be with the Lord forever. Therefore encourage each other with these words. (1 Thess. 4:16-18, NIV)

6. Since the children, as he calls them, are people of flesh and blood, Jesus himself became like them and shared their human nature. He did so that through his death he might destroy the Devil, who has the power over death, and in this way set free those who were slaves all their lives because of their fear of death. (Heb. 2:14, 15, TEV)

7. "He will wipe away all tears from their eyes, and there shall be no more death, nor sorrow, nor crying, nor pain. All of that has gone forever." (Rev. 21:4, TLB)

A person very special to me has died. I feel so lost without him/her. Will we even see each other again?

1. "But now that he is dead, why should I fast? Can I bring him back again? I will go to him, but he will not return to me." (2 Sam. 12:23, NIV)

2. His loved ones are very precious to him and he does not lightly let them die. (Ps. 116:15, TLB)

3. It will all happen in a moment, in the twinkling of an eye, when the last trumpet is blown. For there will be a trumpet blast from the sky, and all the Christians who have died will suddenly become alive, with new bodies that will never, never die; and then we who are still alive shall suddenly have new bodies too. (1 Cor. 15:52, TLB)

4. For what is life? To me, it is Christ! Death, then, will bring more. But if by continuing to live I can do more worthwhile work, then I am not sure which I should choose. I am pulled in two directions. I want very much to leave this life and be with Christ, which is a far better thing; but for your sake it is much more important that I remain alive. I am sure of this, and so I know that I will stay. I will stay on with you all, to add to your progress and joy in the faith. (Phil. 1:21-25, TEV)

5. For the Lord himself will come down from heaven, with a loud command, with the voice of the archangel and with the trumpet call of God, and the dead in Christ will rise first. After that, we who are still alive and are left will be caught up with them in the clouds to meet the Lord in the air. And so we will be with the Lord forever.

Therefore encourage each other with these words. (1 Thess. 4:16-18, NIV)

O death, where is thy sting? O grave, where is thy victory? (1 Cor. 15:55, KJV)

Someone has stolen my valuables and I don't know how I'll replace them. Do I have a right to be angry?

1. "I came naked from my mother's womb," he said, "and I shall have nothing when I die. The Lord gave me everything I had, and they were his to take away. Blessed be the name of the Lord." (Job 1:21, TLB)

2. "A person's true life is not made up of the things he owns, no matter how rich he may be." (Luke 12:15, TEV)

3. For we brought nothing into the world, and we can take nothing out of it. But if we have food and clothing, we will be content with that. (1 Tim. 6:7, 8, NIV)

4. For you had compassion on the prisoners, and you joyfully accepted the plundering of your property, since you knew that you yourselves had a better possession and an abiding one. (Heb. 10:34, RSV)